TO BELIEVE OR NOT

TO BELIEVE OR NOT

Alan J. Delotavo

FreshIdeasBooks
Enlightens, Inspires, Revolutionizes

TO BELIEVE OR NOT

Copyright© 2010 by Alan J. Delotavo. All rights reserved. The author does not allow use of part or reproduction of this book without written permission, except for brief quotations in articles and reviews. Published by FreshIdeasBooks, www.FreshIdeasBooks.com, Canada.

Cover photo, cover design, and interior layout by Alan J. Delotavo. Copyright © 2010.

ISBN: 978-0-9866306-6-8

This book is also available in
eBook and audio book versions.
For this and other books by Alan J. Delotavo,
see www.delotavo.com

For

Believers, atheists, and agnostics alike—that
they may treat one another as fellow travelers
seeking meaning in life.

My son Jed and his generation—that
they may blend a perspective in human life
that's sublime and creative.

WARNING!

The book could be shocking!
But read through and you'll find it exhilarating!

Contents

The Divine Rendezvous	1	9
The Mundane Melting Pot	2	18
Leith: Why I don't believe in God		
Part I	3	24
Part II	4	44
Krister: Why I believe in God		
Part I	5	61
Part II	6	74
Elise: Why nothing is certain		
Part I	7	91
Part II	8	105
Soul-Searching	9	121
The Lonesome Farewell	10	136
The Life-Changing Realization	11	150

This world is so beautiful,
that to insist seeing it only in one color
is a degradation of its beauty and wonders.

1
The Divine Rendezvous

Two men—one with a seven-year-old son—and a woman divinely converged in a Starbucks Coffee in the lobby of Sheraton on the Falls in Niagara.

After sipping his cup of coffee, a man with a book laid face down on the table, asked the man with a child, "What have you there?"

"Oh, Dawkins' *God Delusion*," he shyly answered.

"What about you?"

"Hmm, C.S. Lewis' *Mere Christianity*," also answering shyly. "By the way, I'm Leith."

"I'm Krister, and this is my son, JK."

"Hi!" JK greeted waving his hand.

"Gentlemen, may I join you?" A gorgeous lady in her mid- thirties asked.

"Sure!" the men answered at the same time with the warmth of an instant friendship, as though they have known one another for a long time.

"I'm Elise." The lady offered her right hand for a handshake while holding in the other a cup of coffee whose aroma added enchantment to the ambiance.

"I'm Krister, and this is my son JK." Krister replied, shaking Elise' hands with a warm smile.

"And I'm Leith," he cordially responded, shaking Elise hands with sweet smile and captivating look.

"Have a seat ma'am," JK stood and pulled the chair for Elise.

"Thank you! You're such a lovely boy."

"You're welcome," JK gestured like a matador welcoming a bull to his cloak.

"Look what I've got," Elise said, showing her audio book. "It's a *Wayne Dyer's Audio Collection*. And what do you guys have?"

"It's interesting, we've all got something religious," Leith replied. "I have something Christian, Krister has something about atheism, and you've got something spiritual."

"Are you a Christian?" Elise asked Leith.

"Not really," he replied.

"What about you Krister, are you an atheist?"

"Not really," Krister answered.

"And what about you? Are you into something spiritual?" Krister asked Elise.

"Not really either," Elise answered with a smile, repeating what the two guys said.

"Hello guys, it looks like you're all not sure of yourselves." JK reacted.

They laughed, but the boy's comment echoed deep in their hearts. They stared at him for a moment, everyone telling him in thought, "You're right boy, you're right."

JK understood their actuations and replied, "Okay guys, if you want to be sure about yourselves, why don't you talk about God? Isn't God the only sure thing in this world?"

JK's comment deeply touched their hearts again, this time with something more poignant. While staring at JK again, everyone remembered the turning point in their lives.

KRISTER reminisced about when his mom was in coma and dying. A couple of months before, his dad suddenly passed away also. The busyness of everyday life made him lose forever the precious moments of heart-to-heart talks with his dad before he passed away. Now, he was about to lose those precious moments again with his mom.

Beside her bed, he pleaded in tears for God's miracle. But his mom's condition was just getting worse and worse. The doctor tried to revive her a few times when her heartbeat was slipping. On the third day, the doctor told him that his mom's case was hopeless, and only a miracle could save her. The more he pleaded with God, the more he shed tears claiming for what he believed as God's unfailing promises.

Disappointment with the God he worshipped, worsened by days of sleepless nights and missed meals, was dragging his spirit into the abyss of gloom. It made his body feeble, so that he felt he could no longer persevere in prayer. The more the heartbeat of his mom was fading, the more the pain in his soul was kindling.

"Sir, what shall we do next time her heartbeat goes down? The cardiologist already told you of her condition," the attending doctor asked.

He sobbed. "Just do whatever you think is best," he replied with the foreboding of what would happen, without consenting to end medical intervention.

The evening came, and he went home. He gathered his last strength to pray and all that he could say was, "Please God . . ." Then he realized that instead of pleading for miracles, he just needed to entrust her into God's heavenly care. He did. And the images of *Revelation's* New Jerusalem flashed into his mind and he saw himself hugging his mom and his dad with tears of joyful reunion.

"Thank you God for reminding me that I can still see my mom and my dad again. When that day comes, I'll spend every day conversing with them and letting them know how much I loved them. I'll tell them how very sorry I was for not spending time with them when they needed me most. Bye for now dad, mom. I'll see you again . . . I'll see you again." He fell sound asleep as never before.

Refreshed by a trustful spirit the night before, he awoke in the morning with a beaming soul. "Good morning, heavenly Father, from this day onward I'll entrust everything into your hands. Never shall I relegate you to the fringes of my life again." He spoke to God like a long lost friend he just visited amid his solitude.

LEITH recollected how he finally bid farewell to his once cherished faith. Between one experience and another, Leith was left doubting the divine authenticity of religion. The pressures of doubts and critical-mindedness, compounded by the predicaments of faith-claims had been shaping him into a new breed of free and enlightened person.

"Finally, I'm free! I will no longer allow exploitation of my conscience!" He sighed with great relief, throwing to the garbage the sacred scriptures he valued for so long.

He realized the worship of God had promoted a long list of vanities. A few examples were:

- Political scheming no different from dirty secular politics.
- Racial discrimination and segregation avoided even by the worldly.
- Vicious war (Sunni Muslims against Shiite Muslims until now, Catholics against Protestants, and Protestants among themselves in the past) and unrelenting cold war (believers among themselves) perpetrated in honor of a sublime God.
- Moneymaking that outdid even hardworking corporations.
- And mundane commercialization of heavenly paradise.

"If the followers of religions are who they claimed to be, they could have lived in a more altruistic and helpful life. If the God they worshipped is real, he could have transformed his worshippers into a new breed of noble human species. However, they're no different from anybody else. Why? Because there's no difference between folk superstition, ancient worship of emperors, humanistic philosophy, and present religions. They're all alike—handiworks of people wanting to exploit and control the conscience of those with weak psyche," he realized.

"This day onward, I have nothing to do with religion anymore..."

ELISE recalled the time of her serious depression. She was so dismayed that she was weary welcoming every morning as a bright new day. Often she shivered thinking that the once daddy's lovely and smart girl will break the heart of the father she loved so dearly.

Three times she thought of ending her life. But imagining the father she loved so much, though no longer in this world, grieving the loss of his adored darling, enabled her to transcend such senselessness. She tried her best in each of her three marriages, but they just didn't work. She did all that she could, but they all left her.

She sought the help of pastors, but they offered her nothing more than illusion of divine intervention. She consulted professional counselors, but they just offered her conflicting advices. She called friends and they expressed regrets, but they too were busy coping with their own challenges in life.

"Was it me? Was it them? Or is it just the way life in this world is?" she asked.

To find the answer that's not so much of emotion as reason, she tried faith. But confused by the many competing brands of Christianity, all claiming as exclusive franchisees of God and heaven, she fled Christianity like a plague. Then she tried other religions, and only became more confused. But while searching and not finding the answer, surprisingly, something bright and beautiful was blossoming in her soul. She found new enthusiasm in life, and her depression was waning, until she found herself no longer hurting.

"Who cares anyway? I'll just live my life, one day at a time. Whatever makes me happy and soothes my soul, I'll take hold of it. Whatever doesn't, I'll just let go" she said. "Dad, your darling will stand on her feet again—bold and blithe." She smiled and imagined her dad hugging her and whispering the inspiring words, "You did it my dear! And I'm proud of you."

Realizing that nothing in life is certain and that she still has a life to live after all, she hummed Ray Evans' song "Que sera sera, whatever will be will be . . . " "Whatever my fate brings me—I'll accept with thankfulness and serenity. Nothing in this world is certain anyway. It'll all change, if not fade away. Life is a constant flux—I just have to find quietness while enjoying it . . ."

Surprisingly, JK's invitation to talk about God gave everyone a new impetus. They were all thrilled to share their newfound perspectives on life. No one expected that their seemingly trivial coffee talks could lead to something grand. And the child's nuggets of wisdom will launch them to moving experiences they haven't imagined before.

2
The Mundane Melting Pot

"Okay, let's talk about something that displeases me, yet, ironically, something that I'm enthusiastic talking about," said Leith.

"Oh! Oh! You mean . . . ? My goodness! That's sacrilege my friend, that's sacrilege," Krister replied.

"It's not, my friend," Elise reacted. "What's sacrilegious a-bout something that you're not even sure exists?"

"You mean God does not exist? Look at the world around you, gaze at the expanse of the starry sky at night and see how vast this universe is, yet it's orderly. Look at nature, its design, its wonders, how a seed will grow into a tree. Nature speaks about our loving God who created the universe. Don't you guys realize that?" Krister responded.

"I know this is a revered matter for believers, while a laughing stock to the seculars. So, before we converse about something as delicate as this, let's make a deal to discuss it with intellectual maturity and open-mindedness.

Let's allow each other to speak freely according to one's convictions, reason, and experiences without prejudice.

"How pleasing will our friendship be—when we sincerely listen to one another as fellows in this coffee shop and in the world we live. Who knows, this conversation could be life-changing for us. In this sense, we could have a divine rendezvous rippling through our lives. What do you guys think?" Elise asked.

"Sorry, if I'm a bit impulsive," replied Krister.

"No problem, my friend," Elise responded, while standing and motioning to hug. Krister stood also. "Here's to my dear Krister, ahhh!" Then she motioned to hug Leith. Leith stood. "And to you also Leith, ahhh! Is it warm enough to make us all cordial yet candid colleagues?" They were all smiles, charmed by Elise. A warmhearted friendship blossomed more among them. And they felt connected, like pieces of a jigsaw puzzle that are about to portray a grand mosaic of faith.

BUT is it possible for three people, each with varied worldviews, to listen sincerely to one another and still be friends? Even in our society today, where we value freedom of religion as one of our important social principles, believers and atheists still consider each other mortal enemies. Ironically though, atheists and agnostics can associate with each other with more respect than believers among themselves.

In politics, people change parties. In faith, people die for it. I can't understand how religious sectarianism has become so engrained in people's psyche when they all regard the God they worship as universal. Religious people even regard attending each other's church as heresy and punishable by expulsion from membership. Now what have we here? A believer listening to both atheist and agnostic? Gosh! I couldn't imagine how his church will react. And what about an atheist listening to a believer? How will his fellow atheists react? Will they feel that he's falling back into superstition?

Why don't they just accept that they enrich one another's life, and recognize that no human being is an island? Life is an interconnected and interacting system. Why can't they see one another as part of one universal worldview that enriches human life? Why can't they, as civilized human beings, just be cordially harmonious instead of thinking narrowly and separating one another?

A journalist, doing research on coffee shop conversations thought, while snooping in on the trio's conversation on his high-definition listener.

"May I start then?" Leith asked.

"Sure!" Krister answered.

"Let me expound on why I don't believe in God," Leith said.

"Oh no, looks like this is gonna be serious," JK reacted. "Hope you guys will still be friends after this. Dad, can I watch my movie now?" The guys smiled.

"Sure!" Krister replied.

"And what's that movie?" Elise asked.

"It's my favorite, *Evan Almighty*. I watched it before, but I'd like to watch it again. I love this movie. It's so funny. And I couldn't believe that God likes to have fun too. He makes Evan save the world in a funny way. But why can't God just stay with Evan all the time? Why does he appear, then disappear, and appear again? And why do people have to wear a long beard when they're saving the world? Anyway, may I watch my movie now?" JK said, putting on his 72-inch 3-D iWear.

JK's thoughts amused the guys.

"Okay, let's listen to Leith, now," Elise said. "It looks like this will be the most exciting coffee talk I've ever have," she added.

If not for faith,
what else have we as an anchor in life?

Haven't you realized that religion
is merely a metaphor for human wishes?

3
Why I Don't Believe in God
Part I

Why don't I believe in God? Because when we are just perceptive enough to see the realities behind religion, we will realize that, indeed, there is no God, except the Gods religions created according to their conflicting images. Now let me point out the reasons that made me realize that God is nothing but a human creation.

First, there is a lack of coherent universal management of human life by an all-knowing, all-powerful, and all-present being whom believers called God. Let me share to you this news I downloaded from GlobalIssues.org.

Leith took the note he inserted in Lewis' book and read:

> Today, over 22,000 children died around the world by Anup Shah. Last Updated Monday, September 20, 2010

Over 22,000 children die every day around the world.
That is equivalent to:
1 child dying every 4 seconds
15 children dying every minute
A 2010 Haiti Earthquake occurring almost every 10 days
A 2004 Asian Tsunami occurring almost every 10 days
An Iraq-scale death toll every 18-43 days
Just under 8.1 million children dying every year
Some 88 million children dying between 2000 and 2009
The silent killers are poverty, hunger, easily preventable diseases and illnesses, and other related causes.

Now I have two crucial questions here. First, amid all these sufferings—where are the rich God-worshipping countries? Is God deficient in power to transform his worshippers into altruistic people? Look how extravagant the rich Middle Eastern Muslim countries are, while the rest of their fellow Muslims are destitute and hungry. The money they spent on lavish buildings and lifestyles could have improved the lives of millions of deprived Muslims. Look at the wastefulness of many Christian Western countries while he rest of their fellow Christians are living in abject poverty.

If God has the power to change lives and the worship of God is life-transforming—his worshippers could live a more modest life. Then significantly share what they have to equalize the dignity of human life. But see who are the exploiters and hoarders of the world's natural resources and wealth. Are they not all God-worshippers?

And second, which is the major predicament in believing in God, where is God amid all the deaths of these innocent helpless and hopeless children? What about the millions who lost lives as victims of human brutalities and natural disasters?

"But this is part of the mysteries . . . ," Krister interrupted.

"Krister, no interrupting, please," Elise quickly responded. "Please go on Leith," she added.

If there is a God, where is he amid all this global wretchedness? Believers are ever ready to defend God. Many of them would even argue that God's absence amid tragedies is part of the divine mystery. If so, then why is God hiding from the accountability that defines his tender loving-kindness and being the Creator-God and Savior of humanity? Is it a part of the mystery of God, or merely an excuse of believers to hide the blindness of their beliefs?

I have yet to be a father, but imagine this scenario. People know you as a wealthy and loving dad. One day, your beloved child was in the street shivering in the cold, sick and hungry, begging for food and help to everyone who passed by. But they all ignored him as if he were a social outcast. And you passed by in your limousine, glanced at him and said, "I love you my son." Then you just left him on the street to suffer till death. Somebody asked, "Why did he not save his beloved son?" Those who adore you as a wealthy and loving father answered, "That's all part of the mystery of the father's love."

Elise smiled. Krister was silent.

What a ridiculous proposition! No father who loves his child can do that. Even if he is not the father of that child, any normal human being will naturally sympathize with a child shivering in the cold, sick and hungry. A passerby would usually call for help to save the child's life. Where was God when millions of his children were shivering in cold, if not scorched by the sun, sick, hungry and dying?

Some amusing guys even guessed that after creating the universe, he just left everything in our hands. Others say he's always there, but what is he doing? Just watching his beloved creations suffer and die? Doing nothing, just like the fictitious dad in the limousine? Then it's even inconsistent with the belief that God loves and cares for his valued human creatures.

And please don't tell me, it's because of Adam. What if your great-great-grandfather committed a crime? For instance, stealing an apple from a neighbor's farm because, coming from the tropics, he's curious about how a North American apple will taste. So the state sentenced him with hard labor everyday of his life till death.

Then, after sentencing him, the state also declared an endless sentence to all his progeny. That includes you and your son and your grandchildren. Do you think this is rational and just? But that's exactly what Christianity teaches. And what's ironic is that, this is also inconsistent with the belief that God is just. You see, the Christian concept of original sin is as dehumanizing as the Hindu belief on the untouchables.

Or let's portray another scenario. Probably, believers still need to plead earnestly in prayer, so God could finally be compassionate to the destitute. But I bet, even if all believers in the world prayed every day for blooming crops in the arid African desert, the ending of calamities, and equally restoring the dignity of human life, still nothing will happen. Why? Because believers are just fantasizing about the existence of God. God is merely a psychological tool they created, so they could have an imaginary anchor in life that they, otherwise, couldn't find in the reality of their everyday life.

"Hmmm, you've got a point there Leith. God as a psychological anchor?" Elise reacted, while Leith also realized that he said something that touched his soul.

Second, as I have already alluded to, the absence of divine interventions in human life in particular, and the natural world in general. Even if God is not managing his universal creation 24/7, at least he could have intervened in overwhelming human-made and natural disasters.

Look, for instance, the catastrophes of the early part of the Twentieth Century. You know how many died in World War I? An estimated sixteen million people, excluding the twenty-one million wounded. You know how many died in the 1918 flu pandemic? About fifty million! That's three percent of the then estimated 1.6 billion world population. And the infection spread to a whopping five hundred million or one-third of the world's population at that time.

Were there divine interventions? None! Or probably the death toll wasn't enough yet to awaken the slumbering God. Or perhaps, as in the story of Noah, he just wanted to destroy the world, so he could repopulate it with a new generation of human beings worshipping only one God. And whose God will that be? Will it be the Protestant, the Catholic, the Pentecostal, the Muslim, or the Hindu God? What a merciless proposition then!

If the death tolls I mentioned were not enough, what about the sixty million more casualties in World War II? What about the wanton injustice and cruelty to six million Jews? Weren't the Jews regarded as God's chosen people in the Old Testament? Where was he then when the inhuman Hitler was slaughtering the Jews? Abandoning them as he did with the millions and millions of his other beloved human creatures? What about the more than 220,000 deaths in the 2010 Haiti Earthquakes? The 230,000 dead in the 2004 Asian tsunami? And the more than 800,000 (an average of 10,000 per day) Tutsis killed by Hutu Militia in Rwanda? And many more from both natural and human-made calamities?

Is God incapable of preventing disaster? Is he powerless to end human cruelties? Or did he allow it simply because human beings chose to sin against him? I bet believers, at times, would even rejoice in the tragedy of others not belonging to their religious clan. They would claim tragedy to others as God's judgment for not believing in their particular notion of faith.

But the truth is, there is no divine intervention because there is no God at all. If there is an omnipotent God who created the universe by merely saying a word, why could he not declare, "Let there be no more natural and human-made disasters." It won't take him a minute or two of his infinite time to do that. It's as simple as that. The truth is, belief in God offers nothing more than a temporary and illusory solace for the bereaved. Practical and more realistic grief counseling can even do better than this illusion.

Third, the defects in nature reveal that there is no perfect and all-knowing designer as believers assumed. Aside from the many flaws of human and animal anatomies, look also at the way humans and animals survive. Most animals survive by being predators to one another. What kind of designer is that, who designs his creatures to live by killing one another? And don't tell me it's all about the original sin again.

What do you think a conscientious architect would do if he found a flaw in his cherished project? Just leave his project as is and endanger people's lives? Even sensible human beings will correct the defects in their valued projects, but why not God? It doesn't make sense for an omniscient and loving Creator to just neglect the predatory nature of the creatures he designed and cherished. It's not fun to see divine creatures, human beings and animals alike, killing one another just to survive.

Well, believers would say, God created everything perfect in the Garden of Eden. But who knew about what was going on then? Most believers, of course, assume the Bible came fresh as God handed it to Moses, and as fresh today as it was thousands of years ago. I wish their scholars and educated clergy would just be honest enough to tell their adherents the truth about the Bible. The Bible was the product of compiling ancient manuscripts, each with thousands of variations. And ancient publishers rewrote these manuscripts countless times in the bygone era before photocopying was invented.

Those who chose which manuscripts to include in the Bible were not angels—but people with preconceived notions on what they thought God should think like. They even discarded, if not destroyed, many other ancient writings that did not fit into their mind-sets. Besides, how could we regard the Old Testament writings as the actual account of the origin of the universe when the Hebrew language and literatures just emerged much later in history? And where now was that Garden of Eden so believers could see the prototype of perfect creation? In fact, many Jewish Rabbis even regard the Old Testament stories as allegories of spiritual matters rather than literal history.

Now, back to our imperfect human nature. Imagine the God who loves life, creating human beings who subsist by slaughtering, every day, billions and billions of their fellow creatures. Do these animals feel pain too? Do they also mourn the loss of their beloved families? Of course! But what can we do? That's all part of our imperfect existence that thrives on survival of the powerful. Had there been a perfect Creator-God, it couldn't have been so. Some people even recommend vegetarianism as a more humane way to subsist. But is there enough balanced vegetation to feed us all? Besides, not all species of fruits and vegetables grow in one place.

And another point, what's the purpose of making some places harshly cold and others severely hot—and not all conducive to human and animal and plant life? If I were to design the Earth as a normal rational man, I would make its entire topography livable for all life. Designing one place as fertile and another as harsh could result in both an imbalanced ecosystem and inequitable quality of life.

Well, believers would argue that God originally created the Earth perfect, but because human beings were evil, so God brought floods to destroy Earth and human and animal lives, including plants. Could you bear seeing hundreds of thousands of innocent children drowning because their parents did something bad? What loving Creator-God would do that? And not only drowning them, but also ensuring the next generation will live in an even harsher planet filled with dangerous precipices and treacherous weather?

Even our penal institution provides for rehabilitation. Declaring the regenerating word, "transform," is much easier and more humane than forty days of flood that didn't transform humanity at all. Even the Bible itself tells that after the flood, human beings became evil again. So God's plan, with all his omniscience, did fail after all.

Consider another grave flaw—harshness of nature that threatens our life beyond control. If we were the crowning works of God, he should have given us natural powers to manage the destructive forces of nature. Or just take the destructive forces of nature out. Well, you may say, our natural disasters are human-made, resulting from misdirected industrial culture that abused nature. Yes, we have abused nature and brought curses of disasters on ourselves. But what about the natural disasters long before there was industrial revolution, like Noah's flood, if you believe it to be true?

The truth is, the stories of the Bible are nothing more than ancient myths that believers blindly assumed to be real. Although the Bible contains some spiritual lessons, their stories were not historical facts. Besides, there were several other ancient writings too. But when Constantine institutionalized Christianity, the church leaders he commissioned to collect ancient writings deified some and nullified others.

The deified collection is what we now call the Bible. Of course, the Jews considered the Old Testament as sacred because it speaks about their hopes. Just as the Vedas speak for Hindus, the Tao Te Ching and Analects for Chinese, and the Kojiki for the Japanese. But to adore a particular ancient writing as *the* account of the origin of the universe is nothing but a myth. When one talks about God, either in the ancient or the present, it's all about myths—that are symbolic expressions of human yearnings.

Another painful design flaw—the pangs of birth. If I

were to design the female human and animal species, I would design them in such a way that birth would be more exhilarating than sexual orgasm. It would bring together the emotions of exploding joy—to celebrate life.

"Phew! That would be great!" Elise reacted, jesting, but suddenly turned a bit somber recalling her miseries of losing stillborn babies on two occasions. "You're right Leith, nature is defective. In fact, it's also an abortionist," she silently said to herself.

"Are you okay, Elise?" Krister asked.

"Oh, sorry, yah!" Elise replied. "Go on Leith," she said.

Why let the female species suffer pain while bringing new life on Earth? Should we not welcome life with joy instead of pain? And don't tell me it's because God punished Eve. It's sadistic to assume that. Or don't tell me it was the result of eating a forbidden fruit. Even if the fruit poisoned Eve, where was God's power for damage-control? Or why, as the sole creator, create humans in such a way that you foresee them suffering? Why didn't he ensure the safety and bliss of his beloved creatures?

Think of an engineer creating a bridge that he foresees will cause serious collapse and result in many deaths and sufferings. Or think of loving parents who have a choice to deliver and raise a child in a safe and healthy environment. But they brought their much-loved child to the worst of the ravaged war zones. Then abandoned him.

Before abandoning him, they left a note for him to read when he grew up saying, "We have put you in a war-torn homeland. We are giving you the freedom to choose which band to follow. Choose wisely. If you choose the wrong group, we will come again to punish you. Now live and survive. Your loving parents." This is pure nonsense. I wish believers could just realize how absurd their theology of God and their belief in the origin of human species are.

Even normal human beings can do better than the God characterized by religions. For instance, when an inventor creates something and he sees defects, he doesn't just throw it away. He corrects the defects to make it better, and thus fulfills the purpose he intended for it. Throwing away his handiwork is not just a tantrum, but also like throwing away his being an inventor, because it's part of him and it defines who he is.

Think of the many inventions we have that brought efficiency and comfort to our life, complementing our natural human abilities. If inventors followed the manner of the God characterized by religions, imagine the result of every error inventors commit. The world would be full of abandoned, defective creations. And punishment would await inventors for every error they commit while exploring breakthroughs for bettering human life, as in the story of Eve who was just curious to know more.

> "But can human beings create?" Krister interrupted.
> "Kris . . . ter," Elise reminded.
> "Oh, sorry, again." Krister replied.

I know what you'd like to say. "Can human beings create human beings?" Of course! We mate, and that's a part of our natural procreative power. But if there is a God, he could have prepared a perfect planet for every human being to live, so every time we reproduce we could welcome a new human being into a perfect home. But how many millions of innocent newborn babies, excluding the toddlers, teens, and grown-ups, die every year because of our defective home-planet and defective life we live?

Both natural and human-made calamities always haunt us. He doesn't need to sweat it out. All he needs to do is just say a few words in a few seconds, "Regenerate into perfection!" And bingo! He could save billions of sacred, precious lives and we'll all have new wholesome lives in a suitable and safe home-planet. But the truth is—the Creator-God that religions portray is nonexistent and merely an imaginary being.

Fourth, we cannot confine the cosmic reality in our human understanding. Religious claims about God and creation are claims about realities beyond human. How can we ever fully grasp realities that are beyond the limit of our senses and thoughts?

Think, for instance, of five ants in a Grand Canyon colony proclaiming varied revelations about human beings. One even claims elevation to human status. Each of them promotes their own human revelations. Another describes human beings as the fastest quadruped with a sense of smell greater than all of them combined. And another one tells that human beings created the first and largest queen ant ever with the most virile male ant. Then the human creator placed the first ant couple in the best colony ever, filled with all sorts of human crumbs. So, everyday ants need to worship human beings by biting them hard when ants meet them, so they could bring more crumbs. This may sound sensible for ants because these portrayals reflect their longings and patterns of life.

Religion is like this. It's nothing but a portrayal of human yearnings and archetypes of human life. It's just an attribution of human forms to the ideals of superhuman being, utopia, and how to reach utopia. How could ants ever understand human reality? They don't even have a clue what career, rising and falling realty prices, money, and technology mean. These are all beyond ant-life realities and sense experiences. Look at the vastness of the cosmos. If indeed there is the originator of all realities—that reality is not human, nor can we explain it in human terms.

Yes, believers find comfort and hope in religion, but it's just that—a psychological tool they create to help them cope with the realities of life. In fact, religion is not even as realistic as other practical-oriented motivational approaches, because it always promotes a mystical and illusory way of coping with life.

Further, just think about the religious characterization of God as male. What about God as female? Have you realized that if our human characterization of God is true, what we have is a Creator-God who is like us? He would also have sexual organs and sexual needs, digestive and excretory organs, and so on, otherwise, his body would be useless. Did God create human beings according to his image? Or is it human beings who created God according to their images?

Often religion uses its portrayal of God to manipulate people's conscience. We always hear self-claimed spokesmen declaring their wishes, however exploitive or cruel these are, as God's will. And indoctrinated believers just blindly follow what they assume to be divine declarations because of fear that disobedience will bring eternal doom to their soul. But if we are just reasonable enough to listen to our sanity, we'll discover the truth about the origin of religion. It's nothing but someone's set of mystical theory after deep frustrations and depressions. Just look at the pattern of life of how the founders of religion started spreading their beliefs.

For example, Moses (if he were real), amid his frustration of the chaos and constant rebellion of his people, offered the Ten Commandments as a tool to bring order to his community. Did God write in Hebrew and in stone and speak in Hebrew language to Moses? Or was the story simply an allegorical answer for social spiritual needs?

Did Mary bear a son with God? Or was it a story that Constantine and the religious-political leaders institutionalized to promote the unity of beliefs intended to strengthen the unity of an empire? Did Jesus rise to heaven? People in ancient times thought that above the Earth is heaven, and the world is like a tier of three flat surfaces. They didn't realize, as we do today, that the Earth is just floating in vast space. Did an angel named Gabriel speak in Arabic to Mohamed? Did God tell a bedtime story in Hebrew to Moses on how he created the universe? Did God commission Jesus in Aramaic or Greek to die on a cross to save humanity?

Or like Buddha, after an intense period of frustrations and seclusion, they experienced realization. They realized what they wished for as ideals of life. They reached a heightened sense of awareness of their dormant wishes of how human beings should live in contrast to what they regarded as dehumanizing social context. Then they were able to finally put into words the latent imagery they had been figuring out in their subconscious mind. Those words became the "divine messages" that followers call divine revelations.

Another point, if we take a critical look at the teachings of world religions, we'll discover that they all included previous beliefs. They were innovations of earlier worldviews. Founders and followers then turned their views into dogmas, created institutions out of them, set up societies, and amassed political influences with divine attribution. Then they became recognized religions and powerful competing manipulators of people's conscience. Their power resided in people's conviction that religion holds the rights to the eventual destiny of human soul and the universe. Isn't religion the greatest of all hoaxes in our civilization?

Despite the deception of religion, I won't deny that there are also some good teachings in religion, like teachings of compassion and charity. And it could be noble too, especially when it serves as the practical tool in regenerating our global society. Imagine its social impact when, instead of spreading destructive fanaticism and social segregation, it zealously promotes a productive way of life.

"You're right Leith. I'm also concerned about the dogged segregation of Christian churches. We look at each other not only as competitors but also as mortal enemies. We can't give up our iron curtain because we think that when we become friends, we will lose our God. Our claim of the love of Jesus couldn't bind us as Christ's one universal family of renewed people," Krister commented.

"Thank you for your candid remark," Leith replied.

"Have your coffee first, it looks like it's getting cold," Elise said.

"Thanks," Leith answered.

A pause of silence followed, as if everyone is trying to digest the hard stuff of candid conversation . . .

4
Why I Don't Believe in God
Part II

"Okay, let's keep the ball rolling," Elise said.

Fifth, there is an absence of continuing revelation of God apart from ancient writings. Communication is basic in every relationship. How do you think JK would feel if you, being his dad, talked to him just once a year? Or, although you said you're with him every day, what if, when he wants to converse with you and ask for your help, you don't answer. His teacher asked him, "Does your dad talk to you?" He answered, "I believe he listens but he doesn't talk to me. He just left me a letter after birth, and I have to figure out what his answer will be for all my needs." Is this scenario sensible?

Then, what if he found many other letters, every one claiming the truth and as the genuine letter of his father, but all conflict one another? He sought clarification.

And someone claimed, "I am your father's best friend, and I have spent years studying his letters, and this is what he would like to tell you." Then he met many others also claiming to know his father and to have spent years of scholarly research on his father's letter.

My goodness! Isn't this foolish? If your father is real, living, loving, and with you every day, couldn't he just talk to you? Of course! A real and loving father communicates with his child daily. And they always excitingly converse, and their communication is two-way, interactive, and personal. Even when one is away, they still communicate with each other through phone or Internet.

Well, believers would naturally say that he's God, and not human like us. Besides, he left the Bible or Koran for us to know his will. If he is not human like us, then why do we think of him in human terms and regard our human thinking of him as unquestionable and final? If the Bible or the Koran is God's revelation, why didn't he, in all his omniscience, give us an unambiguous text—so various human interpretations won't confuse his clear message?

Look how Sunni and Shiite Muslims fight to death on who-ever among them has the right interpretation of Allah's will. Christians did that too in the past, and in their cold war in the present. If the God they all adore is real, does he love watching his worshippers shedding blood, just to find out who among them is right about him? What God-believing religions have been doing is clearly creating idols that they can promote as a rallying point to colonize others and spread their self-centered beliefs. What they are offering are collections of guesses about what God, assuming he exists, will say to human beings, and nothing more than that. So with various religious founders doggedly presenting diverse speculations, they fill the world with many conflicting religions.

Is there a personal Creator-God who runs the universe and tells us his will? And if so, what language is he using? It's too culturally bias if he just speaks either Hebrew or Arabic or Greek, and not even the Greek that most Greeks speak today. Why not in English, Cantonese, Hindi, and other languages spoken by many people in the world? And why chat for a bit in the past then hide for centuries when we need him? If God is who he is, as religion portrays him, then he is a poor communicator.

Besides, why only leave ancient manuscripts to guide us through our lives, when our way of life is ever-changing? Life two thousand years ago differs from the present. There was then no genetic engineering offering re-creative possibilities. No space explorations proving there are not three tiers of heaven, Earth and hell in our world. And no advanced medical science offering laboratory-made medicines that keep modern human beings from solely depending on supernatural miracle to cure diseases.

If God is an all-knowing communicator, he could have devised means to communicate effectively and clearly his message, so believers won't misinterpret it. And he should also update his message every time new realities of our life emerge. A sensible CEO would always provide communication updates to employees. Why, if God is real and personal, can't he do it too?

Well, the only reason I can think of is that the religious claims of God are nothing but the products of ancient human reflections. Adherents then reformulated those ancient claims in diverse forms to suit what they variedly thought God should be. Because they had different personalities and concerns about life, they also created conflicting theories and reformulations about God and his will. Just think how confusing God-believing religions are. Not only are the general religious classifications contradicting one another, but also the many sects within each.

Couldn't you just see what folly believers have created to confuse people susceptible to manipulations of conscience? In its truest sense, religion is not about God. It's about spreading one's particular wishes and fantasies in life, borne of deep frustrations. Essentially, religion is nothing but promoting an illusion of utopia amid hopelessness.

Sixth, it's undeniable that human reflection is the root of portraying God's will and identity. Was there an extraterrestrial super-being called God, who can't even communicate with us today, but who conversed with Moses, Jesus, or Mohammed? At least Eastern religions are more honest and less exploitive than Western religions in affirming that human reflection is the root of divine enlightenment. The historical authenticities of the founders of Western religions, except Islam, are still dubious, but let's look honestly and closely at the pattern of how Western religions started.

First you can see the founders' deep frustrations against traditions and what's going on in society. Then out of frustration, they secluded themselves (desert for Moses and Jesus, cave for Mohammed) and went into self-denial (suggesting depression). Finally, after days of intense contemplations—they emerged out of their seclusions with realization of fresh worldviews. They then spread these worldviews as divine revelations.

Eventually on their account of being the bearer of divine revelations, their followers anointed them as the chosen prophets of God. Or, as with Jesus, even God himself. Afterward, when the founders were gone, followers began reflecting and developing their varied views, which suited their wishes and fantasies about their founder's teachings. The results are numerous religious sects that are in constant war with one another.

Ironically though, what followers assumed as a new and divine way of life, also become the potent cause for dehumanizing others. When believers institutionalize their beliefs, it becomes not just a "divine" worldview but also a mundane religion. With institutionalization comes the merger of authority to manipulate conscience and financial and political powers that stir compulsive colonization of others with differing religious beliefs. The results are religious wars that are more vicious than secular wars. Why? Because whether one lives to see victory or one dies to go to heaven—it doesn't matter anymore.

What's foolish though is that zealots just don't realize that all they're fighting for is merely a matter of relative and nonsense opinion. And the utopia they were all hoping for is nothing but an illusion and a tool to exploit their conscience, so religious leaders could fulfill their egotistical agenda.

Further, most religions are merely projections of male-oriented obsession to control the world. It's a means to fantasize fulfilling patriarchal wishes to gain superhuman power to cope with the challenges of daily life. Religion ascribes the power to dominate the world, but rather than to a frail common man, to someone who never fails—the patriarch God. Each of the male-projectors has different specific concerns in life, and varied social and cultural settings where they lived. So the products are various Gods. When one expounds and organizes his projection, the result is a belief that followers eventually institutionalize as religion.

And to control people's conscience, religion uses two major beliefs—God and God's will. God is the character that one wishes to be an illusory superman. God's will is the mandate that one wishes life to be. Then believers venerate a proxy patriarch (God) as the means to mystically fulfill one's wishes in life (God's will), that the projector of a belief couldn't have realized. So what we now have are Gods that are imaginary-beings and Gods wills that are self-centered wishes.

Let's take, for instance, the celebrity preachers proclaiming God's will. Did God speak to them? Or did they just figure out in their offices what to say to fulfill their agenda? Their agenda might include a larger building, amassing more money, expanding programs, expressing their prejudices and notions, and preaching what they understood from their study of other literatures. Or merely teaching what they thought was the meaning of the sacred text they read.

So everything religious is nothing but merely human. That's why I would say that religion is one of the greatest hoaxes in our civilization. Why? Because people just blindly deify one's egotistical, mystical notions as *the* divine revelation. They assume the notion is God's unquestionable voice for human beings. And they just worship the portrayal of one's superman as God.

Could we not just realize how ridiculous it is? Let's awaken to the truth that for centuries we were blind to the subtle exploitations of our conscience by religion. And we dreaded rationally criticizing the Gods we created. Why? Because we are fearful that evil will fall on us in the present and our soul will perish in hell in the hereafter. Of course, there are a growing number of enlightened former believers. But they are afraid to disclose their rational realizations because of foreseen social reprisal. And reprisal is even worse in Islam, where religious leaders are obsessed about imposing their vengeance, cloaked as God's judgment.

That's why I believe that for our society to become more civilized, we should transcend the absurdity of religions. I just can't understand why our modern society still gives preferential treatment to religion. Freedom of religion does not mean granting religion with special status to regulate other worldviews and freedom of expressions.

Although I won't refute the fact there are nuggets of insights from ancient religious texts that we can reapply to our present life. But it's foolishness to institutionalize these nuggets of insights and use them to colonize society with a uniformed mystical notion. This is what Christianity in the past, and Islam even until the present, have been avidly doing for centuries with the inhuman slogan, "Believe or die."

At least Buddhism has taken a more humane approach to religion, with its emphasis on compassion, nonviolence, and contentment in life. Other dignified models are Taoism and Confucianism. Although they are not religions as usually tagged by the Western academe, they offer people something more sublime than other religions. Confucianism offers a practical and noble outlook on human relations based on individual and community gracious reciprocation. And Taoism provides us with a deep eco-conscious worldview that promotes a harmonious cosmic life. These worldviews are also divine, yet they are not as institutionalized as other religions, and obviously they're not colonizers too.

But imagine, for instance, China institutionalizing Taoism as state religion. China then becomes a Taoist Empire, and its mission is to convert the world to Taoism so it could transform the world into a paradise. So now everyone will have to do Tai Chi every day and live in harmony with nature. And by the way, these are not bad propositions either.

I bet Christians and Muslims will exclaim, "This is just ridiculous and tyrannical!" But is this not what they have been doing for centuries? They have been exploiting one of the countless products of ancient human reflections as a tool to subjugate the world. Did the humane God really mandate the religiously-rooted inhuman acts of global magnitude? Or is it just the result of the ridiculous notions and tyrannical tendencies of the delusional spokesmen of God?

"Hmm," Krister reacted.

Probably, if not for the institutionalized and invasion-obsessed Christianity and Islam, what we call religion today would have been a more human and spiritual way of life, instead of becoming institutions for the dogged propagation of religious imperialism.

And *seventh,* the absurd incompatibility of varied claims about God. If there is a God, to be consistent with all religious claims, he should be one and not many. Who then among the Gods of all religions is the true one? I bet all religions, including their thousands of subspecies, are ready to die affirming their self-centered notions. If God exists, he should have revealed himself without contradictions.

An all-knowing, all-powerful, all-present God wouldn't, and just couldn't, allow confusion in his beloved creatures. It would be irrational to enjoy seeing his crowning creation fighting to the death on a simple and easily resolvable issue on who among them is right about him. Seeing his cherished human beings brutally killing one another in a competition for exclusive rights to be his worshipper and to heaven is like enjoying a vicious gladiator game.

Haven't believers realized their madness in sacrificing their lives, money, families, and careers—just for universally incongruent notions of exclusive franchise of an illusory God and heaven? It's difficult for them to awaken to their senses when they grew up with deeply rooted traditions.

When I was a kid, I did hear about faraway countries. But I presumed they were not as civilized as my country and their education and machines were crude. When somebody told me the opposite, I just couldn't believe it. How could it be, when I lived in the best country in the world? Now, as an educated grown-up, I discovered to my amazement that many people in my country still think so; although many universities in what I then called faraway countries have higher ratings than ours.

Why? It's all because of a rooted preconceived notion of cultural superiority. Now, intensify this notion hundreds of times with fear, indoctrination, obsession over life in the future, social pressures and threats, generations of entrenched tradition, and so on. Then what you get is unwavering religious conviction. The conviction becomes unyielding, the belief is always affirmed as the only truth, and the soul becomes enslaved to religion. So a religious soul, however absurd his worldview and way of life is, has only one focus. It's the conviction of being one of the privileged few, among the billions of human beings on Earth, who has the exclusive rights for God and heaven.

If God is wise and loving enough, he should be inclusive, rather than exclusive. Believers ironically teach that all people have freedom of choice, but they offer only two choices, the right way that is theirs, and the wrong way that is others. So who has rights to God and heaven? Christians only? Muslims only? Hindus only? And who among the numerous Christians, and who among warring Muslims? If you just think it through—religion is nothing but plain absurdity!

"Wow! Sounds like you're crucifying Christ again," Krister reacted.

"O . . . oh! Krister, let's not forget our intellectual civility," Elise reminded.

"Oh, sorry, I'm just overwhelmed by Leith's talk," Krister said. "But. . . "

"Okay guys, let's take a break. Leith, coffee or tea? Krister what about you?" Elise interrupted, sensing Krister was about to argue with Leith.

"Your treat?" Leith asked.

"Sure!" Elise replied.

"Let me think . . . hmmm," Leith said.

"Still not tired of thinking?" Krister asked with a bit of sarcasm.

"Okay, I think I want the Gold Coast Blend," said Leith with a smile.

"And what about you my dear Krister?" Elise asked.

"Just the House Blend."

"Sure, sir." Then Elise gently pulled up JK's right earphone and sweetly whispered, "Anything for you my dear?" JK took off his iWear and replied. "Well, what about a creamy chocolate drink?"

"Hmmm, where shall I get it?" Elise replied looking around. "OK, there is it," she said pointing at a fridge.

"How did you find your movie?" Elise asked JK.

"Just great! How was your chat, guys? Did you enjoy it?" asked JK.

"It's great!" Leith replied beaming with relief from the intellectual pressures in his soul.

"Now, it's your dad's turn to tell us what he believes, but before that, let me get your treats." Elise said gently caressing Krister's back to soothe him from the near-shocking conversation with Leith.

"You look like my dad's girlfriend before," JK reacted.

"Me? Why?" Elise asked with a charming look.

"Because you're doing that to my dad's back," JK answered motioning with his hands.

Everybody laughed. "You're such a wonderful boy you know," Elise replied and gently caressed JK's head.

"Okay guys," Elise went to get their treats.

Krister tried his best to quickly organize his thinking. "Leith has got to know this, he just missed the point. I do hope he'll get it this time," he thought. "God please help me," Krister whispered a prayer. After experiencing an intellectual onslaught, he needed strength and zeal to talk about his faith. He was passionate about his faith, but the onslaught caught him off guard. So he struggled to present his faith in as intellectual and persuasive a manner as Leith did. While waiting for Elise, he hoped she would take a bit more time, so he could adequately organize his thoughts. He remembered the classical arguments about the existence of God, but he supposed that Leith would have already known it. So he thought he'd speak from his experience—his life changing experience.

"Nothing is more unquestionable than a personal experience. Who knows, my life changing personal testimony might lead him to find Christ." Krister was enthusiastic. "And after all these years, this could be the time God has prepared for him. I can't wait for him to come back to God," Krister excitingly thought. With missionary passion he waited for Elise to come and start the conversation . . .

Is God, indeed, merely
a metaphor of our patriarchal wishes?

What more sustainable anchor
in human life is there than faith?

5
Why I Believe in God
Part I

Elise came back with an enchanting smile that instantaneously lifted Krister's spirit.

"May I help you?" Leith asked.

"Oh, no! I'm fine," Elise replied.

"Here's your Gold Coast Blend."

"Thanks Elise."

"And here's your House Blend."

"Thank you Elise, thank you much," Krister said. Elise thought Krister was just thanking her for the coffee, she wasn't anticipating anything beyond that.

"Oh, you're welcome. I'm excited hearing what you'll have to say. As excited as I was with Leith," Elise said. "Now, I have my China Green Tip and here's your yummy chocolate drink JK. Now we're all set to go. Let's get the ball rolling again."

"Okay, it's my turn to finish the movie. Dad, remember the song that we used to sing? The last time we sang it together

was when we had a cruise and you woke me early in the morning to watch the sun rising. Then we sang it together, 'A sunbeam, a sunbeam, Jesus wants me to be a sunbeam . . . ,'" JK sang.

"Thank you my boy, thank you," Krister hugged JK and kissed him on the head. JK instantaneously instilled in him the courage to soar like an eagle. Inspired, his mind opened clear, and with zeal, he shared the best exposition of his faith ever. But could this be his last too? . . .

"OK my friends, now let me tell you why I ardently believe in God," Krister said with the enthusiasm he felt as never before . . .

First, the likelihood of our human existence is more viably explained by a belief in God than a belief in fate. Just imagine this. We're personal human beings with complex personality and thinking. We have intricate life and relations. Above all we are living beings. How can we, after all, just come from a nonliving matter?

Just consider this. Would you guys believe me if I told you, a stainless steel spoon gave birth to a human being? Or would a couple who want kids believe me if I told them to just put dirt on a laboratory dish and wait a few years, then your baby will come out of it?

"But . . . ," Leith interrupted.

"Leith, remember . . . ," Elise said.

"That's okay, just make it brief," Krister answered.

"But we're not talking here about a few years, we're talking of millions of years of evolution."

Of course, Leith here might say that indeed a bacterium will come out from the dirt in the dish, then for millions of years that bacterium will evolve into a complex being until it becomes a human being. Okay, say there is a remote likelihood. But what about the likelihood of life coming out from the stainless steel fork? Can life come out from this—a nonliving thing?

He said, showing the fork.

Say we started from atoms, all bouncing around, but could those atoms become human beings by just colliding with one another? It's like saying that, after we drop an atomic bomb new human beings will appear. How can these atoms become the thoughts of our mind? How can these atoms figure out career, sadness, happiness, honesty, integrity, and love?

And not only in origin could we see the likelihood of human existence as more viably explained with the belief in God. But also our life itself, our everyday human life. Where are we going to as a human species? What's our future? What's the future of the planet we live in? Imagine having children and then abandoning them in a desert, telling them that they'll survive because, after some years, they'll evolve into healthy and happy human beings.

Does it make sense to entrust our precious life to the hands of evolutionary fate? No! It's unthinkable for normal human beings to do that. Why? Because we live life with sensible models, with a sense of purpose, with insight into our origin and destiny. We come from our parents; our parents love and raise us, then as we grow we learn to live a purposeful life. Now, take out personal relationship in our everyday life, life becomes void and meaningless. Why? Because, as human beings we are created to relate to one another. And the dignified foundation of our relationship with one another is our relationship with our Creator-God.

Elise was somberly recalling her broken relationships.

To believe that we exist by chance and our destiny is in the hands of fate makes life purposeless. Without God we lack a sense of direction. Without the divine-human relationship providing us the model, our human relationship becomes empty. We'd be like zombies walking every day, living like machines waiting until our batteries die out. Our meaningful life then becomes nothing but mere mechanical operations.

But think about this. Every day we see purpose and meaning in our life. We naturally express love to one another. We face life with confidence. And in times of fear, we have an anchor to cling onto. In times of frustration, we have the Creator-God to call on, like children coming to their fathers in times of need. Remember the feeling we had when, as a child, we'd cry for help, then we found comfort in our father's or mother's arms? It was just wonderful! And that's what we experienced believing in God.

Think how uplifting it is to have a loving and caring parent-child relationship. It's comforting to know that someone who bore us into this world is a living person who cares for us amid the challenges in our daily life. That's what God is to all of us—and that's what unbelief in God couldn't provide.

"Hmmm," Leith and Elise nodded.

Second, belief in God brings about hope and noble values in life, more than disbelief in God. Imagine a life without hope because nobody cares for you?

Elise was somber again, while Leith seemed moved. Krister's talk about relationships struck a divine chord in their hearts.

To whom shall we go to in times of tragedy? When we have tried all possible means but everything kept crumbling? When even our best friends have left us? And we feel we're just alone in this world with nobody to help us amid our hopelessness? And when we're losing our loved ones? To whom shall we go to for comfort and hope?

Elise felt like breaking into tears but was just holding on.

What shall we do? Just consider ourselves not fit to live life because we don't have the power and luck to survive? See the implications of life without God?

"Excuse me, I just have to go to the comfort room," Elise said, rushing out, while holding back her tears. She looked around and nobody was in the washroom except her. She cried, recalling her heartaches from a series of broken relationships. Her beloved dad, to whom she always leaned on for comfort, was gone. She felt so lonely and alone, especially when she needed him most, and he was no longer there. After letting off steam, she washed her face and tried to smile to hide the misery she's been carrying for years.

"Sorry about that, go on Krister." Elise said.

I know each of us has our difficulties in life. Now, if you please just try this before going to bed tonight. Think of your serious disappointments in life. Then pour it out to God. Just open yourself, talk to him like you would to a loving and caring father, and be frank—tell him everything, both the good and the bad.

Pour it all out. Then tell him your dreams in life; what you wish could have been different. If you feel like crying—cry. Anyway, nobody is there to listen to you except yourself and God. I bet I don't need to rationalize to you why you need to believe in God—you'll just experience its significance in your life.

You see, denying God is hard on the soul. Why? Because of the feeling that comes with rejection. When you reject God, you reject the most cherished being in our civilization. Religion is soft on the soul, and is therapeutic too. From the singing of hymns, praying to let off steam, and sharing each other's testimonies of answered prayers. Religion gives us comfort and eases our soul when we are troubled. And these are the benefits that denying God could not provide.

Another is that there is no more sublime source of values in life than God. Yes, there are failings in religion, and I agree there are instances when human beings have created gods according to their images. But you see, faith in God enables us to cherish life in a more fulfilling way. In God we see the models of the ideals of human life and relationship. God teaches us that love, instead of lust or selfishness, should be the basis of our relationship.

"But it wasn't lust, I did it all in love," Elise thought.

In fact, most religions teach us to be kind and compassionate to one another. The cruelties we see in history are not because of religion itself. The root of these is outside religion, usually human injustice. Religion merely becomes a means for people to anchor their hopes while they're fighting for injustices inflicted upon them.

Some people stereotype Islam as a terrorist religion. But look at the peaceful and prosperous Muslim countries like Saudi Arabia, United Arab Emirates, and Brunei.

They don't terrorize the world, nor conquer other countries. All they want to do is enjoy their God-given life. And you don't see a Christian Empire now terrorizing and conquering other countries.

Of course, there are wars among countries with Muslims, Christians, and Hindus. But these wars are not religious in and of itself. The underlying issues are often the result of exploitations perpetrated by secular-minded people. These are not religious people, but secular people with a political and materialistic agenda. In fact, at times they even use religion to hide their true secular identity and wishes.

However, with faith in God, we just don't think of human life as a cheap commodity that just emerged by chance. It's something sacred and precious because God created it so. We see our fellow human beings not just as products of fate, but as dignified creatures of God. Why? Because it's God's will for them to exist and enjoy the beauty and wonders of life.

You see, our perspective of life changes. Instead of insecurity we have faith. Instead of fatalism we have purposeful living. Instead of pessimism we have optimism. Everything in this world looks bright when we see it as a God cherished creation. Our outlook in life becomes verdant rather than withering. If we love life and want to enjoy life, there's no substitute for a faith in God.

Third, God has been an essential and most cherished part of our civilization since it began. Taking it out will result in emptiness, both in our social and individual lives. It's like our biological parenting, we take it out and our human life falls apart. Faith in God or, let me say, religion, is spiritual parenting. If we take it out, our human life falls apart too. Since the beginning of human civilization, we have always had spiritual inclinations. It's part of who we are as human beings. We are not just rational beings but also emotional, social—and spiritual. To take spirituality out of us, to debunk our faith in God, is making us less human.

Look, for example, at the importance of religion in the emergence of many societies. Many nations have historic roots of faith in God. Even China, the historical dynasties that ruled it had their deities. Russia, despite being the former center of the atheistic USSR, is the seat of Russian Orthodoxy. England, US, France, Germany, Italy, Denmark, as well as Latin American and Asian countries—all have religious roots. So did, of course, the great ancient civilizations like Egypt, Babylon, Greece, and others. Take religion out of these societies and they'll lose their rich heritages and historical identities. Instead of faith there would be a valueless culture without deep motivation for realizing the common good of people.

Religion is not just about different ways of approaching God. In its deeper sense it's about us grasping at divine meanings in life amid our human limits. The answers we found, though different, have the same essential role, giving us a transcendent anchor to keep us going in life. So we can find life worth living even amid difficulties. Religion enables us to overcome our difficulties in life. It's one of our indispensable coping mechanisms. And we need it, both in our personal and social lives. Take this essential coping mechanism out, and we will significantly lessen our survival. Without it, our life becomes imbalance and abnormal.

Let me cite practical circumstances here. What shall we do when someone passes away? Just bury the body without, at least, a service that brings about a sense of sacredness to life? Now, we do see many civil marriages nowadays, but mind you, most couples still regard church weddings as more meaningful than civil ceremony. Look for example at the corporate world, the place where people are materialistic. People still believe that a religious ceremony in inaugurating a new building could bring blessings. The absence of religious blessings, on the other hand, infuses an eerie ambiance. Even the materialistic world still leans on a transcendent power to ensure its success.

Throughout history and in all societies, the sense of human need for God is always there. Suppressing or ignoring it is not only spiritually, but also psychologically and socially, unhealthy. Life is not just about what's reasonable or logical. It's also about good feelings, fulfilling relationships, an awareness of our connectedness with the whole creation, a sense of awe and wonder, faith, hope, love, and so on. Life is a multidimensional unity. So we enjoy life and find it fulfilling when it's whole and wholesome.

The talk about enjoying a whole and wholesome life reminded Krister of how happy his life was when his family was still whole. Now, he does enjoy life with his son, but how he wished to have a whole and wholesome family again. The thoughts made him pause for few moments, reflecting on his life.

"Hello, are you there?" Elise asked.

"Oh! Yes, sorry!" Krister replied.

"Something wrong?" Elise asked.

"No, not exactly, I just remember something. But any way, where am I?" Krister asked

"You're beside me, my dear." Elise joked.

Elise and Leith smiled.

"You're talking about your third reason that God is part of our civilization and denying him can lead to an imbalanced social life." Elise said.

"Oh, let me continue with my fourth point after sipping my House Blend coffee," replied Krister.

6
Why I Believe in God
Part II

Now let me point out my *fourth* reason that I believe in God. Worshipping and praying to God provides relief from the deep distresses of human life, and spiritually unites us with the unfailing God. We need God when we are facing the giants in our life. Where else can we go to for help when we have reached our human limits but to the infinite One?

We have to accept that part of our being human is our limited abilities. We are still creatures, though crowing works of God. At times, there are aspects of our life that we cannot control despite how ingenious we are. Despite how advanced our scientific knowledge is, we still can't solve all the mysteries and problems of life. We need someone to lean on. We need someone to whom we can express our distresses in life, or else we'll implode or explode.

Praying to God, communicating with the One who knows all about us, is the most uplifting and empowering means for us to cope with life. It refreshes our will to move on, reenergizes us both physically and mentally, and gives us a fresh outlook on life. Why? Because not only do we have to let off the steam of the pressures in life, but we are also uniting ourselves with our Creator and tapping the divine creative power. We could feel as if the whole universe is with us, renewing our lives, and enabling us to transcend difficulties.

Millions and millions of people in the world can testify what this means, and what God has done in their lives. They can tell story after story about how God worked miracles in their lives amid seemingly hopeless circumstances—from sickness, broken families and marriages, shattered careers, bereavement, and other tragedies in life. And many of them are respected and educated people too, people who are not superstitious at all, but believe that human beings are created with divine purpose.

And not only the so-called good people in society, but even those we call undesirables have found new life in God. These are the people who could have continued living a life that endangered society, but when they found God, their life changed. I could not scientifically explain this, but this experience is real when one believes in God. One of these days, you may try it yourself, and see if it works. There's nothing to lose in trying, you know.

By the way, why do we, as human beings, have a natural inclination to cling to a power beyond us when we face insurmountable problems in life? Why don't we have the natural inclination to just figure it out? Every day it's our nature to figure out how to live, but in crisis it's also our nature to call on God for help. Even those born in an atheist society may not realize this, but indeed in crisis, they look up beyond earth to grasp at something beyond human to help them. As creatures of God, we have the natural sense of spiritual linkage with him, although we express it in various ways. It tells us that by nature, we are worshipful and prayerful to the One who created us. It's the divine stamp in our nature, the stamp that remains in our being both here and in life after.

Fifth, in God we see a powerful motivation in achieving our personal and social ideals of life. Secular motivation alone is not enough to passionately empower us to become noble human beings. Politics and philosophy have tried, but couldn't come close to the impact of faith in God in realizing our human ideals.

Take for example the ideals of freedom in the US. Where did they come from? Faith in God! That's where the pioneers found inspiration from. Yes, the pioneers were not perfect, but as they continued in their journey of faith, they also progressed in their efforts to realize the ideals of national life. Had it not for their faith in God, it's likely that America today would have been much different. Probably it could have become a repressive atheistic society.

Look at the many humanitarian Christian organizations altruistically serving the world. How many millions of people, adults and children, men and women, have found hope in life amid privations, because of the loving and caring Christians? The millions of dollars they spend in humanitarian efforts could have been spent on luxuries that meant nothing except to boost one's ego. But faithful believers spent it instead in a noble cause to save lives. Why? Because of their faith in God. We can never solve all the problems in this world, but at least those who believe in God are touching and changing many lives around the world.

Every time we worship God, we see the ideals of love, compassion, freedom, equality, dignity of human life, orderly society, and a sense of togetherness in creating a paradise on Earth while waiting for the grand restoration of the paradise lost. Every time believers congregate, they celebrate life on Earth, thanking their Creator for its wonders and beauty, while also committing to making life on Earth a reflection of the heavenly.

Secular education alone is not enough to instill sublime human values and ideals of life. All what it can do is promote theories about human life. Secular education produces students knowledgeable of various theories about human life but empty of the passion to make life more fulfilling for all.

Why? Because transforming human life and humanizing the society are not just about intellectual enrichment. It's about transforming the human soul. And only transformed people can become agents of transformation. One of the most sublime contributions of faith in God is transforming human life. A society that believes in God always asks, "Are our acts divine and humanizing?" A secular society can just do anything without the divine reference that serves as the conscience of society. Look what happened to Germany in the Nazi's regime. That's how inhuman people could become when society takes away faith in God.

And show me a truly atheistic society that has both survived and progressed. The USSR fell down. China is not totally an atheistic society for it does recognize religions too, realizing that it can't just wipe it out. Why? Because various religious beliefs are also embedded in its people and history. Faith in God is an essential part of the history of many nations. It's the root of its ideals as free and dignified countries. It defines who they are and where they are going. To strip faith in God is stripping many nations of their history and identity.

Further, faith in God boosts up our efforts in promoting the ideals of human life. To speak about the ideals of human life in mere secular terms, is just like delivering a lecture that enriches one's knowledge but lacks passion for its realization. You see faith in God brings about passions for both personal and social humanization.

Imagine for example, during an emergency when somebody just softly said, "There's fire and we need to leave the building." Do you think people will believe that message? Most probably not, because though the message is there, the expression lacks urgency. That's what happens when we just talk and promote human ideals without the power and expression of faith. With the conviction that God is behind us, our promotion of the ideals of human life changes. It becomes life-changing.

And *sixth*, reality is not just human or merely about what we see and touch, it's larger than that. Often, people rationalize that creation, God, miracles, prayer, Bible stories, resurrection, and even the existence of Jesus cannot be scientifically proven. But you see, our knowledge is so feeble that what we now figure out, we also debunk later with new discoveries. And what we presume as not existing before, we also later recognize as real. Even something as simple as the shape of the Earth, in the Middle Ages people thought the Earth is flat. And by just using our common sense and reason, how can we ever say the Earth is not flat? But, of course, now we know the Earth is not flat but a sphere.

Who would believe in the Middle Ages, for example, that it's possible to talk to each other in a box that can send voices miles away? Who would believe that you can take a virtual painting of a person through what we now call photography? Or even watch the ancient theatrical plays via airwaves? Those were the realities that were beyond human grasp before. But now they're just common.

Before the onset of the industrial revolution, we think of power as literally horse power. Then we tapped dirty oil and our idea of power changes. Now we also know there are still other powers from nature that we could tap, from sound and light waves, to atomic and solar energies, etc. We even know now there is a physical healing power in positive thinking. And some scientists are even now talking about the multiple dimensions of reality. We also know now that black holes exist, where time could possibly be eternal.

And we are discovering other planets and galaxies that show reality is much larger than we thought. Our universe is infinite. Science recognizes that we cannot limit reality to what we usually see and touch. Then why can't science also accept the likelihood of the existence of God?

Some people say that by simply looking closely at all the gods religions are worshipping, we can assume that God is merely a human creation. Look at the stories they've invented, their conflicting characterizations of the nature and ways of God, they're nothing but products of human speculations. But what if there is, indeed, the Creator-God that transcends all religious portrayals? And what if religions see are just the various aspects of one Supreme Being that are not, after all, contradicting one another? We have various religious views because people also have varied experiences in life. That variety of expressions and views about God does not necessarily mean there is no God.

Just as, for example, after our summer break here in Niagara, we'll be expressing in various ways our experiences. Just because we have varied views and experiences about Niagara, doesn't mean that Niagara does not exist at all. Even here in Niagara, there are still countless nonphysical things that we can't all see and touch and are beyond our personal experiences and awareness. For example, there is a variety of emotions that individuals, families, and friends experienced coming here. Simply because we do not have the same experience as others, we can't assume that there's nothing exciting about Niagara. Saying so does not make sense. Those who don't believe in God would even entertain the idea there could be aliens with higher intelligence than us. Why can't they also entertain the idea of a supernatural being with the highest intelligence in the universe?

You see, though unbelievers may think of the creation of the universe by a personal God as myth but the likelihood of humans being intricately created by the Grand Designer is much greater than just emerging by chance. The likelihood of an outer space collision creating a laptop is ridiculous. Even more ridiculous is the likelihood of that collision creating the universe and human beings with more complex natures and functions than a laptop computer.

In fact, it's more mythical than the creation story. Would you believe that out of the big-bang a Rolex signature watch can come out? It's nonsense, right? But this is exactly what unbelievers in God are saying. And remember that living beings and life are more complicated to make than nonliving things. It's much easier to create a nonliving thing than a living being. The likelihood of the existence of a well-designed and complex living being through atomic collision is just absurd.

With the vastness of the universe, we just cannot confine reality to human reality. It's more scientific, to say, as in Star Trek, to go where no human beings have dared to go before. Yes, I agree that Christians based their idea of heaven on the ancient belief that the world had three stories of heaven, Earth, and hell. But that was the worldview before. The essence of heaven is not about the world as having three tiers, it's about the place where the ideals of human life can become realities. It's the prototype of what human life should be.

Heaven, after all, is not just an illusory place. It's possible that somewhere in the universe there is a mega-planet whose topography, ecosystem, climate, and whole conditions are most suitable to perpetuating perfect human life. With our infinite universe, such a possibility is not remote. Einstein's scientific theory of time even speaks of the possibility of eternity. And look, for example, at the longevity many people today enjoyed in the First-World countries because of advancement in medical science and an improved way of life. Some countries even have minimal crimes. The belief of God preparing heaven for human beings is not, after all, that superstitious, it's scientifically probable.

Simply because there are various interpretations of God that seem superstitious, we right away debunk the existence of God. For example, medical science too has its superstitions in the past. Imagine the life-threatening notion that draining one's blood can cure all diseases. Imagine debunking the possibility of a cure for human diseases simply because of the misconceptions in the past.

So why don't we advance our knowledge of God and his creation instead of dismissing it and leaving it in the hands of the superstitious? Imagine what could have happened to medical science today, if we just left it to the hands of those "medical experts" in the past whose knowledge was in its infancy stage. Imagine what travel could be today, if we discarded the possibility of having airplanes because it was beyond ancient knowledge.

You see, the universe is full of endless possibilities, so could we not entertain the possibility of the existence of the highest of all beings we call God? Amid the vastness of our universe, could we not also entertain the possibility of another form of existence? An existence where eternity and perfection are real? Today, for example, we have voice-activated machines. Does this not at least imply the possibility that an omniscient Creator could indeed create our world through voice activation, as in the Biblical creation story?

If we want to think more rationally and scientifically, I think entertaining the idea that God exists is even more rational and scientific than denying it. Why? Because what's more rational is creative, imaginative thinking beyond traditional notions. To be so dogmatic as to say that what we now think is unquestionable, is irrational. The progress of science depends on our motivation that we still have more to learn, more to explore, and more to discover. If we consider what we now know as final and unquestionable, then there's nothing more to learn. And we move back to a nonscientific outlook in life.

I'm not so naïve as to say there are no superstitions and myths in Christianity. I am also critical of people claiming to hear the voice of God mandating them to do something. I don't believe in some healer-preachers claiming to have divine power to heal all sorts of diseases. If this is true, they should go to every hospital in the country and just lay hands to all the sick. Lately, of course, we even heard the news of a marriage breakup of a famed healer. If God is with him, why can't he even solve his marital problems? I also recognize there are many conscience-exploiters. They manipulate people to materially enrich themselves, and promote their delusional agenda.

However, there are also many other preachers whom God have used to bring healing and transformation to the lives of millions of believers. And these are honest and sincere believers who live a modest life with moral integrity. And in times of crisis, they have given us hope and inspiration to move on in life. They helped us get through tough times. Take, for example, Billy Graham. He impacted millions of lives throughout the world, including Presidents of America and many other educated and respected people.

I know there are people who get frustrated with institutionalized religions, like Christianity. I also have a long list of discouragements with Christianity. This includes:

- Racial segregation and prejudices
- Politicking and often manipulative bureaucracies
- Bickering both inside the church and among Christian denominations
- Fundamentalism
- Dogmatism of theologians, as though they are already as omniscient as God
- Cultural imperialism and some other issues

And worse of all, I'm also aware of the tragic brutal-ties Christians and Muslims have done to others and to one another.

But I know and believe that God transcends all these trivial and unfortunate matters that many institutionalized religions have brought. I also firmly believe that God is just trans-sectarian and is the God of all. God, being God, is much larger than any religion can speculate. And simply because I experience frustrations in religion, shall I deny his existence? No! In fact I want even more to explore my faith in God beyond the traditional portrayal of institutionalized religions like Christianity, Islam, and Hinduism. That's why I'm also exploring fresh meanings of my faith in God beyond traditional religion. Give it a try in your life too. Who knows, it might lead you to something life-changing and uplifting also.

"Well, Krister, I thought you were like most Christians I've met that were so fundamentalist, narrow-minded, and judgmental. If Christians are as open-minded as you, probably many secular people will be more interested in giving religion a try. I did try it before, but I was so disgusted." Elise said.

"We'll try it again and see how it works," Krister replied.

"Hmm, now you're beginning to convert us," Leith joked.

"Not convert in the sense of bringing you to a particular

church so I could promise and assure you of salvation. Not that stuff. But it's something more fulfilling and life-changing." Krister replied expressing a fresh passion.

"You mean something like what this audio book is saying?" Elise replied showing her audio book.

"Well, I haven't heard that one yet. So why don't we make a deal? I'll get a copy of that audio book and listen to it. Then tonight, as I mentioned earlier, you guys spend time talking to God and pouring out your serious concerns in life to him. Do we have deal?" Krister asked.

"Okay, we have a deal." Elise replied.

"Now, what do you want us to do then Leith?" Elise asked.

"Think of instances in your life when you tried reaching out to God and nothing happened. And think of the breaking news and events in this world, and see if God is there. Okay, so let's try each other's experiment in life, and see what happens to us afterward. Deal?" Leith also proposed.

"Here's to our journey of personal discovery," Elise said. The trio had a toss. Not expecting that the toss could lead them to unlock the keys to their Pandora's boxes.

"Now it's my turn, and you better listen to me guys. What I say, could change the way you see life as a whole and not just how you see God." Elise said.

What's the answer
to the restlessness of our souls?

How can we ever be certain
of realities beyond us?

7
Why Nothing Is Certain
Part I

Well guys, let me tell you that believing or denying the existence of God are the same. Why? Because they assume that our knowledge of reality is certain and final. We can never fathom reality. What we think is reality, is only what we immediately experience with our five senses. And we can't even experience all of our immediate realities. How can we then be certain of realities like God, heaven, and so on, that overwhelmingly transcend our immediate surroundings? And how can we also be certain of denying God?

Our knowledge and worldviews are ever changing. Is there certain and final knowledge even in scientifically verifiable studies? No! What we now recognize as standard information, we later dismiss as obsolete. We can see this recognition and debunking in medicine, engineering, space studies, and in many other scientific fields. That's why I'm an agnostic. Because all our experimentations and rationalizations are just provisional depending on our individual sense experiences.

One reason I see agnosticism as the most sensible world-view is that our knowledge of God and reality are merely contradictory theories. Despite "scholarly developments" our knowledge is nothing but mere products of our self-centered philosophizing. Why do you think we have varied ideas about God, psychology, philosophy, medicine, and even the origin of the universe? Because different people think differently; different proponents promote different understanding. So what we have is a world flooded with all sorts of conflicting ideas that are nothing but various information and varied ways of looking at realities. They may be sensible to others, but not to everyone. No one can set a specific standard of knowledge for all. Even in our measurements, the world still couldn't agree on one standard.

And belief in God is the leading example of all these ambiguities. Why do we have varying beliefs about God? It's simply because different proponents see God differently. Further complicating the original proponents' teachings are the various ways their followers interpret their beliefs. And the result is the buildup of generations of conflicting ideas with many beliefs and sub-belief groups. Religion has done nothing more than spread more confusion to our already confused world.

What I just couldn't understand though is why, even in our modern civilization considered as educated, we still have people dumb enough to die for a particular view of God. What they're dying for is nothing but a mere theory about God. I'm not just talking here about fundamentalist Muslims but the fundamentalists in all religions, including Christianity. How many Christians have suffered and died believing that their notion of God will assure them of the heavenly paradise in the hereafter?

One of the most life degrading effects of religious beliefs is martyrdom among Muslims, Christians, Shinto in World War II, Sheiks, and others. I don't know why these martyrs just couldn't open up their mind and see the larger reality of life. Of course, because of years of dogged indoctrination, born and raised assuming that they alone, among the billions of people in this world, hold the secret of the universe.

Religion is one of the most deceitful human creations that plagues our society. And it's ridiculous that our civilized societies today still treat religion in special ways, like giving it tax breaks and protecting it from criticism. Can't we just see how religion has been exploiting, as Leith said, not only people's conscience, but also their money? Look at the grand buildings of many churches, mosques, and temples. If religion is that altruistic, they should have modest places of worship that are more natural as the place of worship of the creator of nature. They could have instead spent their money relieving human sufferings.

Just listen to the speeches of clergies. Either they're just mimicking motivational talks christened in religious terms, or delivering messages according to their personal agenda. Did God speak these messages to them, or have they prepared these in their offices using books other authors wrote? And believers just say "amen" as if God has spoken to them. Couldn't believers just awake from their deep slumber of ignorance and insensibility?

It's the same in the academe. We have many religious scholars, even coming from globally respected universities, claiming that their interpretation of God is the most truthful of all, and they all disagree. And I can't understand why refutable universities still have theology departments. I think religion can be more sensible if we change it to lifestyle studies rather than as theological or religious studies. In this sense, people can deduce and find meanings about choices to various lifestyles, rather than focusing on who has the only rights to heaven.

Number *two* point that I'd like to bring about is that, the universal reality is much larger than our tiny human reality. So how can a tiny human being grasp all that is overwhelmingly beyond it?

I'm amused at Leith's illustration of the ant. If we think of the Earth as a speck of dust in this vast universe, our knowledge is nothing but a speck of the universal information too. Imagine, for example, when one claims to proclaim the will of the infinite God. You mean that out of billions of people in our world only that person knows it? That amid our unimaginably countless planets in the countless planetary systems of the countless solar systems in the countless galaxies, only that person knows the mystery of God? That's ridiculous!

And the most ridiculous teaching in religions that I see is God's will. Why? Because, my dear Krister, while claiming God as infinite, it also confines God in a tiny notion of prophets, clergies, and theologians. Nonsense! When can believers ever awaken to the foolishness of religions? I know that even when they realize the folly of religion, it's still hard for them to reject God. Because they're afraid that if they deny God, a curse may fall upon them. Or that their family and friends, and society in general, will reject them too. They're afraid of becoming social outcasts.

Look, for example, at the idea of life in the hereafter. Many Christians, claiming to promote the love of Christ and asserting that God is a loving God, also love to cherish the idea that, someday, sinners will suffer extreme pain throughout eternity. That's one of the most sadistic and ironic beliefs I've ever heard! When we study human history and the dynamics of our civilization, we discover something mundane about religion. It's merely a potpourri of believers' wishes amid their hardships in life and their limited power to control the forces of nature. And, as in the case of belief in hell, their wishes to punish others they don't like but couldn't in the present.

The ideas of God and heaven are just projections of human wishes for rewards and punishments that believers couldn't realize in their present life. These are all symbols of both human personal and communal longings. That's why religion is a myth—the symbolic representation of humanity's yearnings in life. Because believers cannot realize these yearnings in the present, they fantasize about it. And to make it more personal, they project the ideal person to realize it. Thus they have the figure of the all-knowing, all-powerful, and ever-present God to ensure their myths and our fantasies—at least in the hereafter, if not in the present.

Then they make this relative and ambiguous symbolization as the basis of the way they see universal realities. And they cherish this symbolization because it gives them an anchor for their fantasies in life, both in the present and in the hereafter. They treasure this notion so much that they don't want anybody to take it away from them, so they are willing to become martyrs just so they don't lose it. So it's nothing but a delusion, to use Dawkins' term, "God Delusion."

But is religion all bad? No! I also see good ideas and practices in religion. What makes it bad is when people begin institutionalizing religion and making it an exclusive enclave and licensee of heaven. But considering that, although our reflections are relative, they are also the products of human creativity. And they can also contribute, as bits and pieces, in forming our grand, although relative, mosaic of fulfilling human life.

That's why, as I just mentioned, we need to transform religion into lifestyle studies. And consider the varied lifestyle contributions, not as competing but as contributing to a grand synthesis of human life. It's only then that out of one of the products of human culture, we can see something divinely uplifting for our personal and social life. But again, we should not impose religion as the only answer to human needs. We also need to recognize that not only religion, but also other aspects of our culture contribute to the grandeur of human life. These include arts, music, literature, social relations, health and fitness, general education, sports, films, and so on. And together they make up the grand mosaic of our modern human life.

But look at what believers have done to the overall human life. They truncate the rest and impose only religion as the basis of all aspects of human life. This imposition does not only dehumanize our soul and spirit, but also disconnects us from one another, and makes fragments out of our whole and wholesome life. We need to trash the fanaticism and exploitation of the tiny few who claim to hold the secret of the vast universe and impose their delusional notions as the only answer to fulfilling human life.

"Wake-up my dear Krister! Just see the reality!" Elise said while gently tapping Krister's shoulder.

Three, there's nothing absolute about our knowledge of human life and the world. Science changes, our way of life transforms, and our ideas of morality adapt to new situations as we progress in our civilization. Even religious beliefs and practices take on new forms when society's way of life changes due to technology.

If our knowledge of human reality is not absolute, how certain are we of our knowledge about the reality beyond our world? Even in mathematics two elements are not always two. It could be two, one, or zero, depending on the sign that our civilization has figured out. Are there also other dimensions of life when two elements could be thousands or whatnot? I don't know. But is it possible that there are other dimensions of life in the universe where mathematics is different from ours? There could be.

Before we thought that only God could create life. But now with the advancement in biological sciences and genetic engineering, we can indeed re-create life. We can even create sea monkeys. Before we thought reality was just one-dimensional, now we have virtual reality. Fifty years ago we considered our sciences and technologies as advanced. Now, they are obsolete.

Mind you, if Leith can go back to Jesus' time and show the apostles our modern gadgets, like a film projector or even just a microphone, they could be split as to whom to choose as the messiah. People will look at the projected film as the grandest of the heavenly visions. Because while the usual divine vision was private, everybody can see this. You could imagine everybody worshipping Leith as the anointed of God. More so he could project his voice using the microphone. People then will just revere him as the voice of God speaking from the heavens. Let him fly a combat helicopter, (if you know how to, Leith) and even the mighty Roman Empire will fall on their knees worshipping him as a god with superhuman power.

Our creativity enables us to discover and make inventions, shapes fresh worldviews, and brings us to various stopovers in our history. But our journey never ends. Our life and perspective of life is never stationary. Each stage in our history brings freshness to the human way of life. We are not routinely functioning machines, but beings full of life. When we confine our life in a particular myth, we are not only suppressing our creativity, but also dehumanizing our civilization. We become submissive to myths rather than become creative and bold.

Leith mentioned the brutalities of religions. Indeed, religions have brought more dehumanization than humanization in our society, both past and present. History tells of many instances when religious people senselessly punished intellectuals because they did not accept as truth the will of God as speculated by so-called "spokesmen" of God.

The amusing irony though, even to this day, is that while many religiously-rooted universities would like to appear as advanced academe, they still cling to their mythical traditions. Why? They embrace science but impose only the science that promotes their religious beliefs. They still consider religious myth as the basis of modern learning. It's like saying, "Okay, you can do space explorations, but only what reveals how flat the Earth is." "Why?" an open-minded professor may ask. And the rectors respond, "Because it's the truth from God that our clergies have known since they were babies. And if you don't believe it, we shall expel you." Sorry for my sarcasm, but that's exactly what many of the supposedly refutable centers of learning are still today. You can study science, philosophy, and other disciplines, but only that which confirms the veracity of their religious myths.

And why do we see those nonsense fanaticisms resulting in horrible acts? Simply because many lunatics think that what their anointed "prophet" says is the real voice of God, not sensibly realizing it's just the voice of another lunatic like them. Lunacy begets lunacy. Now, tell me of any God-believing religion that has not done any inhuman and lunatic acts in history?

The guys laughed both at what Elise said and the way she said it.

"But if ever Christians engaged in war in the past, it's because they just wanted to defend themselves against marauders." Krister reacted.

I don't think so. History tells us that, in the past, Christians, Muslims, Shinto, and other religiously-rooted peoples did try to convert the world by sword. The truth is, God-believing religions are imperialistic. Even though nobody attacks them, they will still subjugate others believing that their God commanded them to do so—to convert the whole world into their religious empire. Have you watched the movie *September Dawn*? It's horrible! Just horrible! But mind you, this is just a tiny piece of the overwhelming horrors and cruelties religions have brought to our civilizations.

Because of our obsession to be certain with the hereafter, we created many ridiculous myths. And these myths even degrade human life, oppress human freedom, and threaten the sanctity of human creativity. Human life, you know, is more sensible when we see it as progressing rather than static. This makes us grow. Growth and change is the part of our nature, the part of our being. When we continue to freely explore and progress in life without the constraints of religious myths, life becomes fulfilling.

By the way, I don't hate ancient sacred writings, for I also see treasured gems of wisdom in them. What I'm reacting to is the fanaticism toward institutionalized myths. I also wanted to explore ancient wisdom. That's why I'm excited to listen to Wayne Dyer teaching me about wisdom of Lao Tzu. I'd like to learn the ideals of human life from ancient sages so I could relate these to my daily life. And my sages include Lao Tzu, Moses, Jesus, Mohammed, Buddha, Confucius, and others. I'd like to sift the positive universal values from the destructive ones. So I could create a fresh harmonious worldview that is useful in my life without worshipping it as an idol. In this sense, I avoid the usual vanities that religion has brought.

I also see some uplifting values in religion. One of these is common among religions—compassion. In Christianity we find the model of a trans-ethnic compassion as in the story of the Good Samaritan. In Islam it's compassion in the sense of denying one's self to set aside alms for the poor. Another is freedom. Judaism, for example, celebrates the Year of Jubilee and it's also the time for freeing slaves from their masters. About human relationships, Confucianism teaches mutual respect and responsibility. Taoism teaches harmony with nature. Hinduism promotes transcendence from the stresses of materialistic world. Buddhism promotes compassion, nonviolence, and peace.

I'm not against the noble teachings found in religions for, as I said earlier, they are all part of our sublime civilization. What I despise is the lunacy of spreading and heeding the claims of divine will that fanatics use, time and again, to control people's conscience and even horrify our urbane society.

"Now, let me take a sip of my China Green Tip to cool me." Elise said. The guys smiled. "Ohhh . . . Wonderful! It's just so soothing to feel the tea calming our stressed mind and rejuvenating our weary body . . . hmmm . . . . " She sighed gently closing her eyes, letting off the steam that pressured in her soul.

8
Why Nothing Is Certain
Part II

"Okay, now I'm ready." Elise said smiling.

And *four*, if God exists and is omniscient, he should have given us a systematic and unified account of his being, will, and the secrets to finding fulfillment in human life.

Where is he amid all the confusions of beliefs about him? Where was he, for goodness' sake, when I was struggling in life? Leith mentioned communication. No sensible CEO, more so of an omniscient Founder-Chairman of the universe, can just leave his be-loved creatures squabbling to death if who among them has the only truth about him. Or if they all hold bits and pieces of truth about him.

Now let me present to you a more sensible perspective of what religion calls divine revelations. Let's consider, for example, the Torah, the Bible, and the Koran. When we see similar ideas among them, it's not because God had revealed himself to the three chosen prophets. They are similar because the later writings carried over the modified the ideas of the early writings. So we have Christianity that is a Judeo-Christian religion. We have Islam that is an innovation of Judaism and Christianity in the backdrop of early Arabian social context. And we have Judaism that was also influenced by Ancient Near Eastern cultures. So the Old Testament myths, like the stories of creation and flood, are similar to Mesopotamian myths.

And when we study various myths in different cultures and history, we also see a common connection among them. But the connection is not about a unified and directly revealed account of God's creation or will. It's about the common symbols of human longings, mystical attempts to explain the unexplainable, and projections of human ideals.

You see there's a difference between writing an exposition and a letter. Any literate person reading the texts knows the difference between one's expositions of his or her ideas, and a personal letter written specially for a loved one. If you read all the sacred writings, they're nothing but ancient expositions and myths. Of course, in the New Testament we also find letters. But God did not write these letters to his worshippers, the church leaders did, to their members.

If God is as religious people believe him to be, a caring male founder and CEO of the universe, he should have written us a concise and clear letter about him. He should have written it in a special material that will last for centuries. And in a language that everybody throughout our civilizations can understand. Further, the letters should, at least, be in a grand and awesome form, to reflect his grandeur and that of the universe he founded. No CEO of a respected multinational corporation will just leave it to third parties to speculate about what he likes to do in his firm.

Why has God not, personally and directly, left us a clear and unified account of the creation of the universe and what happened afterward? In fact, these stories did not originate from Moses. They came from civilization generations earlier than Moses. Christians, of course, will be quick to say that he did, it's the Bible. But they just ignore the fact that Biblical stories were not direct revelations from God. These stories were myths retold from one generation to another, thousands of years before Moses and Jesus. Christians also ignore the fact that there were many variations of biblical manuscripts, aside from many other similar ancient literatures.

Imagine, for instance, a CEO telling employees that once upon a time, I voice-activated the existence of our company, and bingo, it appeared perfect then! But you guys messed up my company. And despite my having the supernatural power to command things into existence, I just won't do it. Why? Because I have given you the choice to enjoy life in the company or not. For those of you who messed up, eventually, I will punish you for giving me many headaches. I'll wait till the company crumbles to do so. For those who like to live in the company, I authorize you to destroy those who don't, so I can recreate a new company.

Good management? Of course not! This management style is as nonsensical as the story itself. Why? Because if God is a wise CEO and has the power to command the existence of his company—it's more efficient to spend a few seconds recreating it perfectly, instead of just allowing the mess to create further hardships. Or why not create a perfect company in the first place, so it won't endanger his employees?

Ah! What about the freedom of choice? Is it freedom of choice to let the good ones suffer the miseries the bad ones have caused? That's not about freedom of choice, in fact, its injustice. Why not create two worlds: one for the good, the other for the bad? Then just let everyone choose which world they'd like to live in. In this sense, there will be no victims among the good, but only the bad because they choose to victimize one another anyway.

And who are the bad anyway? Are they not misdirected human beings? If there is God, he could have ensured that everybody born is living in desirable ideal life conditions, so they won't suffer defects and do bad. And everyone could just live harmoniously as a healthy and wholesome human civilization. But the reality is, there is no utopia and no human beings can realize it, although we wish for it. So believers create their fantasy-paradise that only their imaginary super being called "God" can realize.

Because they have different personalities and situations in life, they also have different wishes about God and paradise. In their fanaticism, they become zealous in imposing their notions on others. They transform their belief in God to an imperialistic preoccupation. Blend this preoccupation with social and political causes, manipulation of conscience, money, and arms. And the world will see militant fanatics believing it is God's will for them to be horrifying and inhuman. Ridiculous and stupid!

So now amid all the millions of deaths, including innocent children and infants, pregnant women, and feeble seniors—because of religiously-rooted wars since our civilization began—where is God? Nowhere, of course, because there is no God. If ever there are extraterrestrial beings more intelligent than us, they could also be busy coping with their challenges in life, if not just enjoying life. So it's up to us human beings to figure out how we can, together as one human family, recreate a more harmonious and sensible life.

Human life is not about God, it's about us. When we become more human-centered—passionately exploring a more equitable, interconnected, and constructive life—our world will be a better place to live. And we become truly divine. So for me godliness is not about dogmas, churches, sects, theology, and other institutional religious matters. It's about giving birth to a deep sense of sacredness and dignity to the life we all live every day. When we value human life and live by that valuing, we'll see the beautiful and lovely human life blossoming. We complement and enrich one another as we give birth to our delightful garden of life out of our stale global society.

This is more divine for me. And this is even more realistic than just expecting heaven to come from nowhere and in the hereafter, when we probably couldn't enjoy it anymore. True godliness is about making life on Earth more divine and dignified.

"So, Krister, I hope you don't think people like me and Leith as devil's advocates. We too yearn for a fulfilling human life.

Krister, are you here . . . ?" Elise asked while gently caressing Krister's back, thinking that he's dumbfounded. However, Krister was actually staring at Elise with a sympathizing and loving look.

"We're all here, Elise," Leith replied with a smile.

"Thanks Leith. Now let me say my last point."

The *last* point that I'd like to say is—there is no essential difference between the life of believers and the life of nonbelievers. Except, of course, for an illusory expectation of having a preferred reservation in paradise.

How do we distinguish the life of believers from unbelievers? Because others don't go to church and don't believe in God, does that mean that they are murderers, criminals, child abusers, or whatnot? In fact, the same social problems exist among unbelievers and believers alike. Are there molesters among believers? Of course! We can't let the backdrop of clergy reverence make it easy to ignore the issues of molestation in the church. Sin committed inside the church is even more deceptive that sin committed outside the church.

What about fraud? How many churches milk their members while their organizations and clergies squander money on luxuries amid believers fantasizing rewards in heaven? Look at the assets of many churches. They're even more than some multinational corporations who have been providing many livelihoods to people. Just look at the fraudulent belief that giving one tenth of your income to the church will earn divine approval. Imagine paying taxes for a heavenly kingdom? If God is all-sufficient, why does he need people's money?

Let's be candid here. Who needs the money, God or the religious institutions? Can God survive without our money? Can religious organizations survive without our money? Of course not! Religious organizations simply cannot survive without the financial support of its members. They have utility bills to pay, aside from staff salaries, building mortgage, and other operating expenses. But why teach that giving tithes is heavenly when the purpose is mundane? So the church could save more people? Oh, c'mon!

The idea of "holy money" is nothing but a financial tool in spreading one's relative notion about God and life in the hereafter. Of course each church needs financial support. But why impose it by manipulating conscience? I don't know why governments are so ludicrous as to provide tax incentives for promoting theories of God. Religion is nothing but a philosophical business baptized with fear of an avenging God.

If churches solicit donations because they want to serve the deprived and rejected human beings in our society, then it's a noble cause. And I do believe they do deserve tax breaks and even government support for humanitarian reason. But for the state to give churches privileges so they can continue spreading their notions of God and convert more people is just a plain old scam. A scam that even our civilized and educated societies allow in the hallowed name of religious freedom. This is foolish. You mean freedom for religious organizations to deceive people about their various and conflicting delusions of God and paradise?

Now let's take another issue to see if there is indeed a difference between the life of believers and unbelievers. The issue that's close to my heart, my dear friends—divorce. Are believers free from them? The rate of divorce among believers is as common as those among nonbelievers.

Elise made a charming yet sarcastic pause, expressing disgust about the divorce she'd been through. The guys smiled.

What about extramarital affairs? Don't tell me "holy" men and "holy" women are free from it. In fact, some religions allow multiple marriages. It's nothing but lust institutionalized. And why just allow men to have multiple wives, why not also allow women to have multiple husbands? The truth is, religious people are more chauvinistic than seculars. Look at how they treat women. Aren't women regarded as less divine in religion?

I think secular people even have more sensible ethics than the religious ones. Many seculars are family-loving people who just want to live an honest and decent life. They do that because they love life. On the contrary, most religious people are merely trying to live a good life because of fear of punishment from a judgmental God. Imagine being punished by an eternal and horrifying hell. They're scared to death, so they have no choice but to be good.

Further, when secular people become generous and charitable, they do so because they like to. When religious people do it, they do so calculating their rewards in heaven. It's a selfish giving, rather than an altruistic one. So it doesn't matter whether one is a believer or not—what matters is the life one lives. And no religion can assure people that it can transform them from something bad to something good. In fact, at times religion even makes people worse.

Of course, there are instances when criminals become believers through preaching, even when still in jail.

But remember, these are people with imprisoned souls. And as human beings, they want to get out of their miseries. It's not about religion itself or the power of God that changes one's life. It's about people, consciously or subconsciously, wanting to change. It just happened that religious preaching was there as a tool in changing their life.

Transformation of life is not even exclusive in one's religion or church. Change happens to people in many other places and avenues. And not necessarily brought about by God mediating through a church or a preacher. For example, what about the lives changed through counseling sessions with a secular counselor? Is God there too? If it is, then there's no need to confine him in a church. Some friends who converse and share their problems in a bar also experience transformation of life. And that's an irreligious place to experience conversion of human soul.

What about love and hatred? My goodness! I found no other ironic place than religion where the claim of love is coupled by hatred. In religion we see the love to God often deeply entwined with hatred to others belonging to different religions or sects. In fact, because of the love of God, religious people would destroy others. Why? Because religion is the most self-centered and exclusivist of all our social institutions.

It's self-centered because sectarian beliefs become the center of human life. And people who don't live the prescribed life are regarded as outcasts who should be converted either by choice or force. It's exclusivist because it regards itself as the only way to God. Other ways are regarded as heretical and devilish. This blindness in religion is so grave that when believers do devilish and horrible acts, they ludicrously think it's divine. So we could even see more murderers among religious fanatics than resolute atheists or agnostics.

The only superficial difference I see between believers and unbelievers is the delusion of paradise in the hereafter. While many secular people just live every day, one day at a time, believers see every day as moving toward the end. And the end that they look forward to is the destruction of the world and their exclusive salvation. What a pessimistic outlook on life and an egotistical delusion.

So I hope we are all sincere in listening to one another and setting aside our prejudices. After all, we belong to one human family, and we are all as human as one another, regardless of our perspectives in life. And as a family, think how beautiful life will be when we join our pieces together in the portrayal of a fulfilling grand mosaic of our human life and civilization. Instead of fragmenting it, why not make it whole? We all have our prejudices based on our experiences and sense perceptions. But, together as one human family, when we transcend our prejudices and become open to the all-encompassing blend—we can create a more pleasant and harmonious life.

"Wow, I'm astounded at what you said. It seems you're speaking outright from the heart, like me and Krister. And it looks as if we are all moving toward a new synthesis in our individual life. I wonder, what will be the impact of our coffee talk to each of us?" Leith comments stirred up one another's defining moments.

"So guys we have heard each other, what next?" Elise asked.

"Are you guys staying for few more days?" Krister asked.

"I'll be!" Elise answered.

"So am I," Leith said.

"Well what about another coffee tomorrow?" Elise quickly said. "And it will be my treat again. But this time, instead of just saying what we think, why don't we ask and clarify each other's viewpoints, so at least we can have a clearer picture of how to blend our perspectives on life?"

"That sounds good." Leith replied.

"But no argument, just clarification. No debate, just a friendly conversation. And most of all—the willingness to sincerely listen to one another." Elise added.

"Sure!" Leith said.

"That will be great!" Krister said.

"Is JK still watching his movie?" Elise asked. "Looks like he's asleep, either bored with the movie or tired waiting for us."

The guys laughed.

"JK time to go," Krister gently tapped JK's shoulder slowly waking him.

"Oh, how was it Dad?" JK asked.

"Fine!"

"How about your movie?"

"Well, Dad, it's my third time to watch it and every time I see it, I discover more fun. It's so funny when God suddenly appeared, then suddenly disappeared after telling Evan what to do. So guys don't be afraid when God suddenly appears telling you how to become a superhero!" JK said with enthusiasm.

The guys smiled, thinking through the words JK said.

"And another one, don't be afraid when something strange happens, because that can be good too." JK added. "And don't forget to help one another. Don't leave someone without helping. And remember ARK means 'Acts of Random Kindness'."

The guys smiled again, amazed at how a child's simple words could awaken their awareness to life's precious lessons.

"You're teaching us many lessons JK," Elise said gently,

caressing JK's head.

"Thanks," he responded. "Yeah, now I can see around! C'mon Dad, I'm excited," JK stood and grabbed his dad's hands.

"See you guys tomorrow." Elise said

"And thank you, Elise, for the coffee." Krister said while leaving and waving his left hand.

"My pleasure," Elise lip-synched.

"Thanks Elise," Leith said while hugging her.

"My pleasure, Leith, my pleasure." Elise hugged him too with the warmth of her heart. "I hope we opened Krister's mind," Elise said.

"I hope so too," Leith replied. "See you then," he bid Elise goodbye. Elise waved at him with a sweet charming look.

"Hmm, interesting guys," the journalist thought. "They all speak with the same passions. But what will happen to each of them? That's interesting to see . . ."

The grandeur of the mosaic of life unfolds
when we bring together our answers
to the enigma of our existence.

9
Soul-Searching

ELISE went to Fallsview Casino to further let off steam the restlessness in her soul. At least she vented her viewpoints earlier. But there is restlessness in her soul. After a couple of hours in the Casino, she went back to her hotel room. Lying on the bed and staring at the ceiling she reflected . . .

What am I really seeking for? . . . I don't know . . . I know Leith and I wanted to change Krister's notion of religion, but he has some points too. I still don't believe in God. The likelihood of the existence of aliens with higher intelligence is much greater than the likelihood of the existence of the God of religion. There could be some beings in other planetary systems with more capabilities than humans. But even if they exist, I doubt if they understand human life.

What about angels? My, my! That's a common myth Christians borrowed from another culture they call "pagans." Religion is nothing but a myth—expressions of the symbols of wishful reality. But where shall I go to find the answer to something I can't understand? I don't like religion. I don't like believing in God. I despise the certainty of knowledge. But it seems what I'm looking for is something that . . . I don't know . . .

Don't tell me Krister, you're beginning to convert me. No way! I'm still sensible enough, despite my frustrations in life. But could I, indeed, be seeking something mystical in life? Something beyond what's rationally sensible? Well, it's not a bad try. After all, there are many facets to human life. Just as I'm not certain of knowledge, I should not also be certain about denying the existence of other realities.

Gosh! Don't do that Elise . . . But should I not also be certain about denying the existence of God? Oh! No! I'm confused . . . OK, say there is the highest being in the universe. But I don't think that I'm that foolish as to accept the Gods of religions. Besides, who among them shall I choose? There are just too many of them, so many forms, and nothing but speculation.

What's the answer I'm really looking for in life? And why am I looking for the answer when there's nothing certain in this world anyway? Yes, as far as information and knowledge, there's nothing certain, but I need to find something sensible in my life. I need something that, at least, gives me rest from my restlessness.

Or probably I'm just restless because of all my frustrations trying to find a lasting and happy relationship. Imagine no more intimacy, no more sweet kisses and exciting romances, no more arms to hold me, making me feel secure, no one close to talk to and share sweet nothings with at bedtime. Am I just looking for a new relationship or something beyond that? . . . Oh no! Elise don't lose your mind, don't you ever lose your mind. A mystical relationship with an imaginary being just isn't the answer. I couldn't deal with that, that's not a real person but a mere fantasy.

What I'm looking for is a real person, a real touchable relationship . . . But I have already tried it several times and all what they gave me are heartaches.

"Ah! Hmm . . ." Elise sighed then smiled.

What about flirting with either Leith or Krister, or both, and see who falls in love with me. What if it's Krister? My goodness! He'll be preaching to me all day and all night. I couldn't imagine myself attending church services and singing those funny hymns, or having a "holy disco." That's funny, the church trying to draw disco-loving people to

God? They're full of gimmicks nowadays just to convert irrational people, you know. Besides, how can I take care of a child? That's too much for me. Cooking food, waking up early in the morning, getting his child ready for school, attending school meetings, and so on. These are just stressful for me. I can't live with that.

But Krister looks like an honest and sincere man, different from all my exes. He's just a simple man, and being a single dad—that takes much patience, sincerity, and self-sacrificing love. Oh how I wish I could find a man like that. But why look for somebody else, when he's already here? I can spark something beautiful. Besides, the way he looks at me tells me that he likes me. He's sort of having a secret "love at first sight" thing with me. What if we have dinner together say in the Skylon Tower? That's the perfect place to spark a romance amid the awesome ambiance of the grand Falls . . .

Now what about Leith? Gosh! Both of us have compatible worldviews, but he'll give me more restlessness in my soul with his disbelief in anything beyond material. Besides, he seems carefree as I do. And yes, I'm carefree most of the time, but I'm also searching for something fulfilling and stable in life. However, Leith is a suave professional guy, formal yet charming and classier than Krister. He's the guy who can go with me to parties. You know, the guy who looks so good in a tuxedo, as well as in casual wear. He'd be somebody I could be proud of to introduce to people as my dear husband.

But he also seems restless and mad about something I can't understand. As if he has an unresolved anger over something, probably God or whatnot. He's mad at religion like me. And although we're one in trying to change Krister's mind, we're still strangers to each other. We don't know each other's secrets. He doesn't know why I became an agnostic, and I also don't know why he became an atheist. It looks like both of us have hidden secrets behind our masks.

Gosh! What shall I do? ... Let me try my audio book. And well, I promised Krister to try what he suggested before going to bed tonight. Just so I can tell him honestly tomorrow that I did it. No harm trying it anyway. Okay, now let me listen to this guy and see if something good can come out of it ...

KRISTER and JK went for a ride on the Maid of the Mist. They were both awed by the grandeur of the Falls. JK kept on clinging to his dad's hands, a bit scared of the enormous pressure of falling waters. JK stared at the Falls and the mist that rises from it. Krister though, on seeing families enjoying the adventure and fun together, became a bit sulky and began reflecting . . .

How I wish my family is still together. I can imagine the fun we could have here. Yes, I'm happy that JK is with me, but how much happier I would be if my family is complete? And where were you God, when I needed you most? Where were you when I lost my calling, and my ex-wife left me for another man? You see, if you really care for your children, you should have answered my prayers.

At times I would just assume that what happened in my life is your will. Often, after many prayers though, still undesirable events happen in my life. And I just rationalize that it's your will anyway and something good could still come out of it. I believe you exist, but do you really answer prayers? Do you really work miracles in our lives today as you did in the past?

Forgive me for my doubts, but honestly there are times when I think that after you created us, you just left everything in our hands. Have you left us in the hands of fate? Have you abandoned us? Forgive me again, but many times, I just prayed to you because I'm afraid that if I don't, a curse will fall on me. My prayers are now becoming mechanical, like letting off the steam of my fears and anxieties in life instead of that intimate conversation with you. Because you don't seem to care for me anymore, and don't seem to answer my prayers at all.

I haven't ever prayed for luxuries in life. Remember years back, when I was pouring out my heart to you to heal my mom, as you did with many others while you were still on Earth? But you didn't. Yes, I did have peace of mind then, but probably it was just because I learned how to accept reality and did not really experience your miracle. Remember also when I was ardently praying for a happy family? But what have I? Thank you at least, for giving me JK and he has been my inspiration since then. He's the only human being who keeps me going. He's the only human being I have learned to love. And thank you for letting me understand the depths of the father's love to his son as it was for you and Jesus.

But look at these happy families together, there are countless numbers of them in this world and many of them don't even worship and serve you. You know how faithful I am to you. And please don't make me like Job. That's not a desirable life for believers—it's like a theatrical show of the gods of Olympus. And I believe that you're the God of life and not a god of death. But why can't you just give me a whole and happy family again? JK needs the love of a mother too. He also needs the friendship and fun of a brother or a sister. What will happen to him when I get old and he has no sibling to lean on? For years now, he's been dreaming of a brother or a sister. And I also need the love and support of a tenderhearted wife.

Please forgive me my God, I don't mean to dishonor you as the Lord of my life. But I believe that you understand my struggles in life, just as Jesus had been through all the pains we have as human beings. I pray that you understand me. I have nowhere else to go. My friends and family members have abandoned me. They are just too busy enjoying life, if not coping with their challenges also. I and JK are just alone in this world. And now, it seems that you're leaving us too. Please heavenly Father . . .

You know many times JK has been asking for something from me, and although I said no at first, later I said yes. I believe you're much more than I or any loving father on Earth. So please, I've been pleading with you to set me free from the bondages that have imprisoned me for years. Please give me a fulfilling career and a happy family.

Remember when I first accepted you, years back when I was in college? I sincerely said in my heart that all I want is to serve you the rest of my life. Now it seems that you have rejected me. Then when I thought I was ready for family, I dedicated our lives to you and fervently prayed that all I wanted while serving you is a happy family. But you have allowed both my commitment to serve you and my wish to have a happy family to be broken into pieces. Those were not bad prayers. They were not materialistic wishes. They were worthy prayers. But why? ...

Please God, help my unbelief. At times, I think that people like Leith and Elise have reasons to think the way they do. I still could not let go of my faith in you because you're the only anchor in my life. JK trusts that, with me as his dad, he can just make it through life every day without worry. He's not anxious about the future. Could I also be like him to you, as my heavenly father? But please show me the reasons to think so. Show me even just a bit of the miracles that you have shown to others.

Please Jesus, you know what it means to be human. You know what it means to worry, to have broken dreams, and being left alone. I know you can sympathize with me. So please hear my cries. Just say, let it be, and it will be done, as when you created the universe.

I hate to say this and my conscience too trembles at this thought, and forgive me, but I'm losing my faith too ... And I need to release the pressures in my heart; otherwise, I'll implode. Please show me the sign that you are real and you care for me. I need you to strengthen my faith, please, my God and my Savior. Strengthen my faith . . . and show me the way . . .

"Dad! Look at the birds. They must be enjoying the Falls too. Probably they're taking a shower on the mist. That's it, that's what they're doing." JK interrupted Krister's reflection. Krister jerked when JK called for his attention. "Wow! That's great!" Krister said.

"Oh no! Are we going right into the Falls, Dad?" JK asked, holding firmly his dad's hands again.

"No! We're going there but we're not going to sink. C'mon, put on your raincoat's hood properly and fast." Krister said.

"Oh no!" JK let loose of his dads hands and hugged Krister tight instead.

"That's okay! C'mon, face the Falls and I'll hold you tight." Krister slowly turned JK around to face the Falls while holding him. "See, every thing is safe, everything is okay . . ."

"Wow!" JK exclaimed experiencing the Falls up close.

Just before leaving the wharf, Krister looked back at the Falls as if saying to God, "Thank you God, what next? But just hold me tight . . ."

LEITH went up to the revolving Skylon Tower for the lunch buffet.

He was awestruck by the grandeur of the Falls. "Wow that's awesome!" he said. "I could have invited Elise with me," he thought. He gazed on the Falls for few minutes and began reflecting . . .

Where did, indeed, this grand universe came from? Of course, having a God as religion characterized it is a nonsense proposition. But what about if indeed there are the highest categories of beings that are so scientifically advanced that they could create living beings from nonliving things? Could this be more probable than the big-bang? But, if supreme beings exist, where did they come from?

Elise is right. It's just maddening to think about the origin of all realities. I don't need to solve this other-worldly mystery. Besides, what's the importance of this in my everyday life? Even if higher beings spawned life on Earth, they don't care about my daily life. If they do, they should have made life on Earth easier, peaceful, and equitable.

Or probably they just spawned life and left it to evolve into higher species. So some life became plants, other animals, and then, human beings, the highest of all life to have evolved. But again, what about the very origin of all realities? Where did those higher beings that spawned life on Earth came from? Oh! My goodness! This enigma is taking away my fun in Niagara. I even missed inviting Elise for a dinner.

"Man, I just missed it," he said with regrets. "Probably I'll stay for another day; perhaps I'll meet someone of the same flock."

Krister seemed so sure about what he was saying about God. I still remember the silly time when I was like him. But Krister's belief in heaven and Earth seem to play a role in psychologically enabling him to face life with confidence. But why at times do I have an instinctive phobia about dealing with my crisis in life? Anyway, it's not just me, it's common among all human beings.

Probably what I need is just a close friend. Or maybe it's time for me to marry. It's been a while now, since I had an intimate relationship. It's like I don't even know how romance and intimacy feels like anymore. I need that gentle touch, the lovely caress, the enchanting bedside talks, and that enthralling physical union of two people in love with each other. Oh my! When can that happen again?

Why don't I try that online dating with Russian or Ukrainian ladies? Man! They're just gorgeous and fine. They're family-oriented too and less demanding. But who among them is real amid all those online dating scams? If only I could meet them directly, right in Russia or Ukraine, that'd be fine. Why don't I go there for vacation? But where do I go to meet them? Agencies? No way? They'll just scam me. Besides, how sure am I that the woman I meet through an agency is not abused and may carry over her trauma to a marital relationship? Well, at least I could save one of them. But this is not the time for me to play hero. That will just complicate the simple life I'd like to live.

Hmm . . . but wait a minute. Why not try the church? Yeah, those fundamentalist Christian churches. You know. At least, I could be sure that with their fundamentalist and conservative way of life, they could be decent women. That could be a great idea. At least I could have more peace of mind marrying a Christian, or any religious woman, than a secular carefree woman. A religious woman has conservative values in life. And she is likely more faithful and loving to her husband than a carefree one.

But how could we have a compatible family life, when I don't believe in God anymore? And she will be going to church every Sunday, and my goodness, that will be the last place I'd like to go! Imagine the stress of sitting in the church, wasting your time, listening to a delusional "prophet" claiming to be the spokesman of an illusory god? No, it won't work! I'd enjoy loving the woman, but I'd be afflicted with a psycho-religious disease.

Why not just engage in a casual relationship with no strings attached? I'll just have fun without marital commitment. In this sense, she enjoys, I enjoy, and when it's time to part, we can bid goodbye to each other without heartaches. That could be a good idea. Love, after all, is just a misnomer nowadays. It seems like love has already become obsolete. Many nowadays just marry to have companionship and support, aside from meeting each other's sexual needs. Then when they get bored with each other, they explore others more exciting than their spouses, till marriage just breaks down. And kids suffer. Good, if both couples wanted divorce, they just let go of each other. But often the innocent party is devastated. And life and careers are shattered by the wanton folly of the other partner.

"C'mon guys!" A gleeful woman motioned to her jovial family to come. "This is where we sit. Remember, its Mom's treat this time, next it will be Dad's."

"Wow! Dad, look at the view. It's just awesome." A teen child said with excitement. Her dad peeped and said, "Okay guys let's get food first, then we'll enjoy the view while eating."

Leith's attention was caught. He continued reflecting . . .

Wow! What a happy family! I think I'm just making a negative generalization about love and marriage. This family looks happy. Look at the excitement they all have. How I wish I too could have a family ... Perhaps I was engrossed laying aside religion, particularly Christianity, and have forgotten to savor happiness and contentment in life.

I rejected religion because I wanted freedom from my oppressed conscience, but it seems I'm beginning to sow pessimism in my soul too. That shouldn't be! That's not the road I'd like to travel. All I want is just a happy free life. Happy, because I enjoy life to the fullest, despite some human imperfections. And free, because I can realize my true being without the constraints of superstitious beliefs. But how can I achieve it? Where do I start from here? I've got to start from something else ...

After pausing for few minutes, he was excited realizing something.

That's it! That's it! I need an anchor in life, my home base, where I start and come back to for reference. Krister is right, and I also said it, human beings need an anchor in life ...

10
The Lonesome Farewell

"Well, here we are again. I've got to watch another movie again. I hope I won't fall asleep this time waiting for you guys." JK said and they laughed.

"So what movie do you have today?" Elise asked while gently caressing JK's back.

"It's Winn Dixie," JK answered.

"Winn Dixie, as in the store?" Elise asked.

"No, it's 'Because of Winn Dixie,' and he's a dog," JK replied. "It's a cool story because people don't like each other at first because they're different. But later they became friends and accept one another. And everybody's happy. I hope you guys will be friends, though you're different. Right Dad?"

"Sure, my boy!" Krister answered.

JK responded with a thumbs-up. The guys smiled realizing again the nuggets of JK's wisdom. It's the wisdom they wouldn't have listened to if it were an adult telling them.

"As I promised yesterday, it will be my treat again. And I hope that you'll remember me as well as our interesting coffee talks. I hope something good can come out of these. I hope this rendezvous can someday help us find the answers we've all been looking for. So what shall I get for you, Krister?" Elise asked.

"Okay, let me try tea this time. Just any tea you can pick."

"Looks like even in drinks, you're now beginning to explore alternatives," Elise said smiling sweetly. Krister smiled too, while realizing that, indeed, he has become more open to other views in life.

"And Leith?" Elise asked

"Okay, let me also try tea. The Wild Sweet Orange."

"What about you my dear JK?"

"Still the same. The yummy creamy chocolate drink."

"Looks like you guys are having tea. So why don't I try a something different?" Elise looked around. "Ah! Also the yummy creamy chocolate drink. This will make me feel younger than you guys," Elise joked. And the guys smiled.

"It looks as if we are all into the business of exploring alternatives," Leith joked back.

Moments later Elise came with the treats. "Wild Sweet Orange for you, Leith. And here's an exotic Zen tea for you, my dear Krister. And here's JK's and my bottles of extra creamy chocolate drink."

"Okay, now let the ball roll for the last time," Krister butted in. JK put on his iWear and watched his movie while drinking his chocolate every now and then.

"You see guys, I don't have all the answers to the issues you brought out against religion. But let me just point out something here. First, religion and faith in God has been a part of our way of life. From education to health care, and even to national anthems throughout the world. The leading centers of education in the world have religious roots too, from Harvard to Princeton and from Cambridge to Oxford. So are the many leading hospitals in the world, from Catholic to Protestant. You see, religion has been the driving force behind many of our educational and health institutions. Because religion provides a powerful drive in making human life better.

"And, of course, as I mentioned yesterday, religion is also an essential part of the founding of many nations. And not only Christian nations, but also those of Muslims,

Hindu, Shinto, Confucians, and other religions. So what will you do with religion that is embedded in the existence of one's nation, culture, and identity? We just couldn't take these out because we couldn't rationally and concretely prove the existence of God. Imagine what will become of these countries when you take religion out. There will be chaos, identity crisis, and eventually destruction of society and people. You see, religion is not just about beliefs, it's about people. You take religion out; you also destroy people's lives.

"Okay, say, let's take religion away, but what shall we substitute for it? Philosophy? I don't think philosophy has that deep, sublime, and sustainable driving force to shape people's lives. Something merely theoretical just passes away like a fad. A philosophy may gain people's attention for a while, but in the long run, it lacks that conviction and life-changing passion. There's no substitute for religion. Philosophy couldn't comfort one person, let alone a nation, in times of sorrow. Philosophy couldn't bring about the courageous spirit that religion instills.

"Whom shall we substitute for God? Our country? And substitute faith in God with the spirit of patriotism? Well, in many societies patriotism is always connected to faith and love of God. We just couldn't be rational all the time because when we face crisis in life, reasoning just does not work, but faith does."

Leith smiled with a bit of sarcasm at Krister's talk.

"We need something spiritual to help and guide us in times of our deepest needs for meanings and inspirations in life. Even doing transcendental meditation couldn't provide it. All it does is provide a temporary denial of reality. But faith in God brings both serene acceptance of reality and hope beyond tragedies in life. So if we talk about humanization, there's no better means for humanizing people than religion.

"Of course, I recognize there are undesirable fanatics in religion, but anywhere you go, there are always bad apples. It doesn't mean that since we see a few rotten apples, that we now stop eating apples. And it doesn't mean that since there are varieties of apples that we now just throw apples away without trying them to see how good they are."

"You mean you're also open to trying varied forms of religious expressions other than Christianity?" Leith asked.

Krister was caught off-guard by his comments and Leith's question. "Umm . . . yeah! Why not? I see something good in every religion. So I'll just pick up the good ones and leave the bad ones," Krister replied.

"So are you moving toward a new religious synthesis? You might end up creating a new one. Not a bad idea though, if it offers the world a fresh and synthesizing faith. Let me know someday when you find a fresh alternative to our present stale religions," Elise said.

"Well if ever I'd like to promote a new integrative religion, I'd like to start first from Christianity. Probably, an integrative Christian faith that synthesizes the good in various denominations and offers Christians, a fresh and transsectarian Christian faith. Anyway, even if I come up with it, I foresee I may not have success spreading it."

"Oh? Why the pessimism? Where's your faith?" Elise asked.

"Well you see, the Christian academe and churches are discriminative. They specify what racial voices they would hear. They won't allow contributions from other people. Just look at the leaders and thinkers of Christianity, and you'll see they're racially selected. I could say the secular world is even more open to diversity and inclusion than Christians. Christians have been persistent in suppressing diversity and inclusion, particularly with ethnicity and gender. It's part of their selective outlook on faith. They always fear that when they become open they'll lose their idols and even God.

"You're right Elise, most religions are discriminative. Most Christian bureaucracies and academe are racially selective. They regard other people as less intellectual or less divine.

"You see, I have to accept that I, too, have frustrations in Christianity. It's one of the most racially segregated religions in the world. Christianity in North America, particularly the evangelical and Pentecostal forms, is nothing more than holy ethnic religious spas. A place where segregated people can come every Sunday and try to make each other feel good as members of a holy band.

"I and JK, amid the challenging times in our life, have been hopping from one church to another, mainly Caucasian evangelical and Pentecostal churches. They vary from liberal to conservative. We were seeking an inclusive and welcoming church. But we found no difference among them. They were all consistent in their sectarianism and wily rejection of the contribution of what they tagged cultural minorities," Krister spoke, expressing his regrets about an undesirable Christian practice.

"So, now you realize that, indeed, if God is true, he could have transformed Christians into more fair-minded people. Or at least Christian faith could have made Christians more ethnically and gender inclusive. Do Christians not believe anyway that all people came from one couple created by God in his image?" Leith reacted.

"I'll be honest to say that indeed there are also important issues in my faith that I'm struggling with. But I believe God will show me the way, one day," Krister answered with faith amid uncertainty.

"Now Krister, let me ask you this question. How do you find certainty in life?" Elise asked sincerely, while also trying to prove Krister's ingenuity in providing faith-answers.

"My faith!" Krister answered. "I have faith in God that, although I couldn't find answers to many of my serious questions in life, he will someday, at unexpected moments, show me the way."

"Is this not a blind faith?" Elise asked.

"No. I find no such thing as blind faith. Faith believes that something you don't see and couldn't concretely figure out is possible and will be realized in a miraculous way. When we reach our limits, God intervenes when we believe in him."

"But give me something more concrete and more practical." Elise further asked.

"Well, when you're worried about life, leave it in God's hands. Let go of your worries, and just have peace of mind and face life one day at a time. Remember that if God cares for the lilies in the field and birds in the sky, he will also care for you. It's not about philosophical truth; it's about faith, faith that God will perform miracles in our lives."

"Hmmm. I've already learned to be carefree in life. Why am I beginning to be anxious again?" Elise thought.

"Well Krister, back to the issue of synthesizing faith. Do you think that all religions are talking about the same God?" Leith asked.

"That's what I thought before. I realized though, each religion is talking about different Gods. God in Judaism is the one almighty Creator who has chosen Israel as his people. In Islam, he is the God who rewards faithful Muslims. The Christian God is an incarnated divine-human being and the Savior of all who become Christians.

The Hindu God is an abstract God to whom everyone who is free from the cycle of birth and rebirth will eventually merge. The Shinto Gods are spirits of family ancestors. A Taoist doesn't think of God like western religions but the universal principle of existence to which we should all harmonize. Of course, Taoism also has a mixture of spirit worship. Buddhism has no God, though those who have reached enlightenment can also help people gain enlightenment."

"Now do you see that indeed religion is full of human-made idols?" Leith asked.

"But you know, despite their different beliefs about God, there is still something common in it—that God does provide salvation to human beings. Now the important question here is not about who among the world religions has the true God, but who among them will God accept? I believe that God understands all people, and whether he will accept one form of religion over the other, that's his choice. It's up to him to judge, not I. What I'm just concerned about is how faithful I am to him.

"But that's me. That's how I see faith. And that's what I believe. We're all different, and God deals with us in different ways. Honestly, I too have my serious struggles in life. At times, I also question God. Sometimes, I'm also uncertain of my future, despite my faith. I'm still human, you know, subject to doubts and flaws. Sometimes, I also wonder where God is. But my hope is that someday, when we meet again, we'll all be excited to share each other's discoveries in life."

"Well it looks like you're trying to bid goodbye to us

now," Elise said. "I'd like to let you know that I enjoyed our conversations. And this has been helpful to me. Our coffee talks have opened my mind to some possibilities too. And I hope it's the same for you and Leith."

"Thank you too, Krister. Thank you for listening to me, too," Leith offered to shake hands with Krister. Krister shook it lightly. "And thank you, Elise." Elise raised her hand in a friendly gesture of saying you're welcome. Elise smiled, deciphering Leith's look. Leith then turned to Krister to continue saying something important.

"I know it's hard for you to listen to me, but you're kind enough to. You're more open-minded than many believers I know. I know most believers would think of people like me as satanic or evil, but we're still good human beings, you know. It's just that we found a different path in our search for meaning in life. Because we're different doesn't mean that we're demonic or whatever. We're as human as others who have different worldviews. We also value the dignity and sacredness of human life.

"And I too have my struggles in life. At times, I'm also wondering where to go. At times, I'm also hoping that somehow I could get hold of something miraculous to help me make it through life. But, of course, I sense that one day, I'll also find happiness and contentment in life. You know, that kind of life when every day you wake up, you're thankful that's it's another wonderful day; instead of dragging yourself to another challenging day. I hope I'll also find the answer I'm looking for. Thanks again, Krister, it was a pleasure meeting you. And I hope you'll also explore other alternatives in your search for meanings in life, as we do. And here's my card. Let's all keep in touch." Leith said while giving his business card to Krister, then to Elise.

"By the way, if you don't mind, what's your PhD in?" Krister curiously asked.

"Ironically, theology!"

"Theology?"

"How come?"

"It's a long story. To keep it short, after teaching theology for years, I finally arrived at the crossroad where I realized theology is nothing but the trash of egocentric thinkers."

"Wow! And here's mine too." Elise said charmingly handing her card to Leith, then Krister.

"May I also ask you, if you won't mind, what's your PhD in?" Krister asked.

"Anthropology. I was fascinated at how human beings developed their fine civilization. But I ended up becoming the CEO of our property holding company when my dad passed away.

"Oh! And here's mine, as well." Krister also gave his card.

"And you also have your doctorate. And what's this?

"Doctor of Ministry."

"Now I know why you speak like a minister. So which parish are you serving?" Elise asked.

"Ironically, I resigned a couple of years ago. I couldn't accept any longer the power play inside the church and the skeletons hidden in the holy closets. And I was also fed up with sectarian dogmatism that separates and isolates Christians from one another."

"Hmmm," Elise and Leith hummed at the same time.

"Well . . ." Elise hugged Leith, then Krister. Leith and Krister also hugged each other. At once, they realized their coffee talks had drawn them like longtime best friends. And they felt lonesome saying goodbye to one another. They also felt as though they all belong to one grand mosaic of life.

Elise gently took off JK's iWear and said, "My dear JK, I guess you still have much time left to see around."

"Oh, good it's done! Now we can go to the Bird Kingdom. Have you guys figured out what it is that you really want in life?" JK asked. "Hmmm," the guys hummed in chorus, with the hunch that indeed something life-changing is about to happen in their lives.

"Let's go, Dad," JK grab his dad's hands excited to go to the Bird Kingdom. While on the way out of the hotel JK noticed something, "Dad, I saw that guy again. I also saw him yesterday. And he seemed to be listening to your conversations. I think he's up to something."

"Which guy?

"That guy?"

The guy glanced at them too.

"Never mind, let's go, Dad," JK said.

11

The Life-Changing Realization

KRISTER—

While on the Greyhound bus going back home, Krister reflected...

"They're right . . . I've been harboring this pressure in my conscience for years, now it's time to let go of it . . ." He took a deep breath, then slowly breathed out, as if breathing out the miasma in his soul. "At last, I'm free!" he sighed. "No more God of fear and bothered conscience. No more sectarian God. Only the God that's caring, friendly, and ever-partnering."

Then the image of Jesus tenderly holding a lost sheep in his arms flashed in his mind. "It's only you and me, my boy. It's only you and me . . . But don't worry, we're not lost, and we can make it, for we have a Friend . . ." He silently yet boldly said looking at JK leaning on his shoulder sleeping. Then he hummed the song, "What a friend we have in Jesus . . ."

LEITH—

On the plane back home, while gazing at the sky, Leith reflected...

"You're right Krister. I came to enlighten you, but you enlightened me instead. Yes, I need an anchor in life... But it couldn't be an anchor in the gods of religions though. No, not a mystical anchor but, yes, still a relational one... Yes, it's the anchor based on fulfilling human relationship—family—the family that loves, cares and supports one another. And also relationships with my friends. I need to nurture and enrich these relationships. These are my anchors in finding fulfillment in life.

Well, it looks like it's time to make phone calls and visit people I've missed for so long. But most of them are believers, and how do I fit it? I'm sure, in time, they will learn to accept who I am . . ." Leith smiled anticipating his future.

ELISE—

Elise, on the night before leaving Niagara, sat on a lounging chair in her hotel room overlooking the magnificently lit Falls. While watching in awe, she began thinking...

"You're right Krister, I need to let go of the pressures within me. I needed time to meditate and have peace with my soul . . . Yeah! Now I get it! Meditation! But what kind of meditation? Hmmm . . . Not the meditation of conscious focusing. Not the meditation of conscious emptying. But that's it—the meditation of harmonious life with the universe. But no, not just meditation but a way of life.

"Now, no more philosophical answers and endless confusion—but a daily harmonious living with nature and my fellow human beings. Could it be that this is what I've been seeking? Wow, I'm on my new journey in life . . ." She was excited.

THE JOURNALIST—

Laying on his bed and staring at the ceiling he reflected . . .

"They all spoke sense, if only they could blend their views, they could create a breakthrough, a fresh worldview. But if I were to blend it, what would it be . . . ? Hmmm . . .

"Yes! That's it! And that's who I am! I am a believer who thinks there could be the originator of reality because reality must have a beginning. If there are different beings on Earth (humans and animals); different beings of animal species from microbes, worms, clams, fish, ants, monkeys to dolphins; there could also be different beings in the universe. And there could also be the universal Supreme Being.

"But the nature of that being is not human. And its reality is beyond the human world. The God religion created is very human and clannish. It's nothing but an idol. So I am also an atheist who does not believe in worshipping an exclusive portrayal of the originator of realities. Because the reality that originated all realities could not be limited to exclusive religious personification. In human terms, we may call it the Supreme Being, but its nature is beyond human understanding. So I'm also an agnostic who understands that nothing final can be said of the originator of all realities.

"But what will I substitute with religion and God?... That's it!" He was excited.

"Um!" He jerked when the doorbell rang. He stood and opened the door.

"Dad!" His excited eight-year-old son hugged him, followed by his six-year-old daughter. He hugged and kissed them too.

"Honey!" His wife hugged and sweetly kissed him.

"How did your snooping go?"

"Well, interesting, shocking, mindboggling, but stimulating!"

"But honey, what happened here? The room is messy. And look at yourself. You look like a weirdo with a beardo."

"Are you a Santa Claus, Dad?" His daughter asked. His wife laughed, so did he.

"Tell me what happened to you Hon."

"Well, I've been trying to solve the mystery."

"Like Nancy Drew, Dad?" His daughter asked?

They laughed again.

"Well Hon, you can't stretch yourself trying to solve the mystery. Mystery will just unfold itself every day. C'mon, have yourself a bath, dress up and shave yourself. I'd like to see the suave guy in you. Honey?"

He smiled seeing his wife's charm and foreseeing the revolutionary contribution he's about to unfold . . .

There's more to a butterfly's life
than crawling as a worm.

Thanks to:

- Ingram, Amazon, and CD Baby for equally opening the global book market to unrepresented voices.
- The Christian churches and colleges in which I sought refuge, for letting me realize that there's more to faith beyond sectarian enclaves and racial biases.
- Shirley Parr who lovingly volunteered to instruct my son when I couldn't afford a tutor.
- The freelance editors who are partnering with me in FreshIdeasBooks and helping me believe that publishing for the under-represented voices is possible.
- To Serenity Software Editor for helping polish my manuscript.
- Sheila Sproule for editing my manuscript so I could present my valuable message to my readers in a clear and polished manner.

I am _____
       (Your Name)

And I am proud to be an/a:

_____
(Atheist, Agnostic, or Believer?)

Because:

_____
_____
_____

www.ingramcontent.com/pod-product-compliance
Lightning Source LLC
Chambersburg PA
CBHW061655040426
42446CB00010B/1743